"*Brad Worthley makes the strongest case yet that* ADD *is a Gift, not a Disorder. His irresistible enthusiasm leaps off the page. He is persuaded that it is the school and the workplace that should change and accommodate the creative "outside the box" type of brain, and he offers practical solutions for how to do that right now. This book offers specific recommendations for managing the negative self-talk which may have cropped up after years of frustrating experiences and negative feedback, and incorporates intimate first-person perspectives of living with the challenges and delights of the* ADD *spirit.*"

David D. Nowell, PhD
Licensed Psychologist
Clinical Neuropsychologist
www.DrNowell.com

"*The most striking feature of Brad Worthley's book,* "ADD is a Gift, Not a Disorder: If you don't have it, you should get it" *is the passion and conviction and joy of the author. Brad really LOVES having ADHD, and this is an important message for parents of ADHD kids or for ADHD-ers themselves. Instead of preaching doom and gloom or advising parents or individuals to accept a level of defeat, Brad Worthley highlights, with stories from his own life and the lives of others, the fearlessness, creativity, and passion of those of us who are "gifted" with ADHD. This book will give hope and optimism to families and it will reassure and encourage those adults who haven't yet found their drive or purpose. Enjoy! You will come away happy to be so awesome!*"

Margit Crane, M.A., M.S., M.Ed.
Award-Winning Author, Educator, and AD/HD Game Changer
www.GiftedWithADD.com

D0113151

ADD is a Gift, Not a Disorder

If You Don't Have it, You Should Get it!

Brad Worthley

ADD is a Gift, Not a Disorder

Copyright © 2013 Brad Worthley

Printed in the United States of America

ISBN: 978-0-9770668-1-0

The content of this book is also available as a keynote speech.

Please contact the author for more information about the keynote speech, interviews, speaking engagements, books, DVDs or audio programs:

Brad Worthley International
12819 SE 38th St #375
Bellevue, WA 98006
(425)957-9696
Brad@BradWorthley.com

Please visit our website at www.IamNotDisordered.com

Book layout and design by Stephanie Martindale
Cover design and graphics by Mathes Design

This book is dedicated to two incredibly gifted people in my life whom I love very much;

*The first is my son **Tate Worthley**, who showed signs of creativity and ingenuity from a very early age.*

The education system branded him a "C" student, but the real world gave him an "A." Today, he is very successful, and the signs of creativity, ingenuity and fearlessness shine on.

*The second is my father **Harold Worthley**, who I always wanted to be like, and I still aspire to his greatness.*

I was always in awe of his ability to think through any challenge, his ingenuity to fix anything, his creativity to build a better mousetrap and his entrepreneurial passion. The "C" grades that the education system labeled him with were an insult to his true intelligence.

Both of these fabulous people are great examples of people who have the gift of ADD.

Contents

Acknowledgments

I want to thank a friend and adviser of more than 20 years, Lee Holloway, who insisted I write this book. It had been on my mind for many years, but I convinced myself I was done writing books for a couple of years (I had three up to this point). I had even told my wife, Melanie, that I would be able to focus on other parts of my business this year because I was not going to write a new book. Lee, you are one fabulous salesperson to convince me that this was an important issue for me, and I thank you for your tenacity and gift of intuitiveness.

I also want to thank my fabulous wife, Melanie, for her partnership, not only in our personal life, but in our business life as well. I once heard it said that behind every great man is an even better woman; they were not wrong. Her support of my passions and life's journey is unwavering, and she is a huge part of everything I present to the world. She is one of the main reasons I have an extraordinary career and life.

I truly appreciate the people who offered to share their stories at the end of the book, in chapter 13, which is titled "Other People with The Gift." They opened their hearts and souls by telling how ADD has impacted them as they grew up, and how it affects their lives today. Many of you who read this book will find their stories relatable and see yourself in their shoes. This book and their stories may help explain your journey through life as well. You never know, you may be one of the gifted ones too!

I want to acknowledge the tremendous gift of Kathy Mathes (www.mathesdesign.com) for her talent as a graphic artist in designing my book, DVD and workbook covers. I want to thank Stephanie Martindale who always found time to help me make my dreams come true with the layout of my books. I am also grateful to the many people who lent me their eagle eyes for the editing process, including Betty Compton, Kathy Compton, Jim Brown, Joyce Daman and the final eye of Lisa Cosmillo. Thank you all!

Introduction

I am not a doctor or psychiatrist, and I do not have any plaques on my wall that recognize my ability to survive a grueling education process. I am not a 4.0 GPA (Grade Point Average) student and did not get to speak at any graduation ceremonies, even though I think it would have been pretty entertaining if I had. However, I do consider myself somewhat of an expert in the gifts of ADD (Attention Deficit Disorder) because I have been living with the gifts for 59 years.

In high school, I was a "C" student, and I graduated with a 2.47 GPA. My parents would have given anything to have had me make the honor roll in high school. It only required a simple 3.0 grade point average, and I could have had my name printed in the local newspaper for all to see. However, even with my best effort, that was not to be. The only time my name was in print was when "poor work-slips" were mailed to my parents, letting them know my grades had just dropped from a "C" to a "D." Any mail that came from my school to our house was not going to be good news.

I could not understand how the kid sitting next to me in high school could be so socially inept, unable to throw a football, barely tie his shoes, pick his nose and eat his boogers, but he could get straight A's and be heralded as our best and brightest. There were many children in my school who fit that mold (sans the boogers), yet there were people like me who were social rock-stars, great athletes or creative souls that seemed to have it all, except good grades. I felt smart, yet every time I took a test or got my report card, I was reminded that I was not smart enough with my "C" average.

My "C" average was a result of having grades like:

- English = D
- Math = D
- Science = D
- PE = A
- Art = A
- Wood Shop = A

I did poorly in the memory classes, where testing "smart" was a quantitative method. However, I did very well in classes that required physical prowess or artistic talent where the scoring was qualitative and left in the hands of the teacher's discretion. When all was said and done at the end of each year, somehow, even with my best effort, I was still a "C" student.

I was at school every day – I never skipped a day of school in my life, but I still got mediocre grades. I actually tried hard to do well in school but consistently struggled and could never understand why. I had friends who did well in school, who seemed to know exactly what they wanted to get a degree in and what they wanted to do when they grew up. It terrified me that I didn't know if I could even qualify to go to college, yet alone know what I wanted to be. I felt like a ship without a rudder – isolated – like I was the only one who felt that way.

I hid my grades from my friends and did not talk about it because it was embarrassing to be a "C" and many times "D" student just able to survive even the most basic classes. I ended up taking art, wood shop, metal shop, auto shop, photography and other classes that required ingenuity and creativity – where I could excel and get passing grades. But I struggled in the classes that seemed to matter most to the education system, like English, Math and Science. I even failed a class titled "World Problems" in my senior year and had to take a night class at our community college in order to make up the credits so I could graduate with my class. No one but my parents knew it because it would have been humiliating for anyone to know that I almost failed to graduate with my class.

Even with my mediocre grades, I felt like I was smarter than my grades painted me to be. I felt like I had skills and talents that were not being recognized by the education system – I felt they were missing the measure of my intelligence, but there was no one to turn to who would listen to my pleas for mercy. Does any of this sound familiar? Does this sound like your life story too?

I am writing this book from a unique perspective, from one of a person who believes they have discovered many of the gifts that come along with ADD. The most predominant are the gifts of creativity, ingenuity and fearlessness. It is a perspective that might be challenged by academia and some in the world of psychology, but I am OK with that. This book is about my journey and discoveries, not theirs (let them write their own damn book ☺). Today, I truly believe I have gifts that many people do not have, and for those that know me very well, they would support me in my belief. Am I perfect? No. Do I make mistakes? Yes. Will I continue to make mistakes? Yes. Will I learn from my mistakes and grow from them? Yes.

Even though the education system did not think I was good enough, I have created seven companies since I was 20 years old. I built my dream home on the highest mountain in Bellevue, Washington overlooking Mount Rainer when I was 39 years old. It had a 10-foot-tall waterfall that ran down my bedroom wall, and electric curtains that opened to a 180-degree view of the world. It had a wine cellar, sound-proof media room, and television that appeared from a pedestal at the foot of my bed. I have owned fabulous cars, many boats, including a stunning new 47-foot motor-yacht, a summer home and as of the writing of this book, I own four other homes.

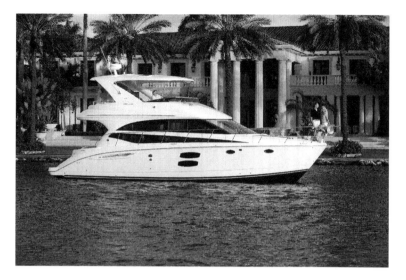

Our 47 foot motor-yacht, "Making Miracles"

I live an extraordinary life filled with incredible joy and happiness. I truly believe I achieved many of these wonderful things in my life because I have a gift; the gift of ADD. I am not dumb, I am not broken, and I do not have a disease, ailment, malady, syndrome, sickness, illness or disorder. What I do have is the gift of creativity, ingenuity and fearlessness that many people do not have. I consider myself to be incredibly lucky and embrace my gift every single day. It has made me who I am and allowed me to flourish in my business and in my personal life.

I have come to believe that it is the traditional public education system that is broken and damaged, not me. Who in that system made themselves God by telling people with a good memory that they are the only smart ones and that they are worthy of the only accolades? Who decided that the gifted ones were the ones who could retain whatever they heard or read and recall it upon demand when taking a test (the gift of mental regurgitation)? Yes, they have good memories, but does that truly make them smart?

Maybe those of us who tried hard in school and only got C's are the gifted ones. Maybe those who struggled in school and chose to protect themselves emotionally by dropping out and walking away from a broken traditional public education system in frustration are the gifted ones. We are the entrepreneurs who are building businesses, hiring people and stimulating the economy. We are the ones who do not take "No" for an answer and push through in tough times with our tenacity, making powerful decisions that keep the dream alive. We are the innovators who drive change and motivate people to think about how things could be done differently.

We are creative, we are ingenious, we are fearless and we are ADD. We are not broken, the system is. We do not have a disease or a disorder – we have a gift. We are not victims; we are fully in charge of our own destiny. We are completely capable of greatness. We are ADD!

Chapter 1

Full Disclosure

I am not a doctor, so this book is not written from a clinical or technical point of view. There are many great books already out there that cover ADD very well, so there is no need for me to write from that perspective. I am an entrepreneur, business consultant and professional speaker, who lives with the gift of ADD. I have lived with the frustrations of ADD when I was a child (primarily frustrated with getting low grades) and been blessed to live with the gifts of ADD as an adult. I discovered that I had ADD when my son was diagnosed with it when he was in junior high school.

My son's journey was a photocopy of my own journey through the education system and the frustration of feeling smart but having my self-image crushed by poor grades. After my son's diagnosis, we tried different medications for him and varying doses for a couple of years, but it was a guessing game that was almost more frustrating than having ADD itself. This must be why they call doctors' offices "practices" because it is not an exact science, and sometimes, it is a lesson in futility. After months of "practice," my son finally made the decision at the age of 13 to simply go the distance without medication. We honored his decision, even though, at the time, we did not know if it was the right decision.

In our research of ADD, we found out that it was primarily considered genetic and passed down through the gene pool. Out of curiosity, I asked my father if he knew what his grade point average was in high school and he did not remember. With his permission, I contacted the high school where he graduated and found that he had very similar grades in school to me and my son. The classes that he excelled in were art and shop classes, very similar to those of my son and me (my dad also played in the school band, in which he also did very well). All three of us struggled in what I call "memory classes" such as reading, writing, math and science. My father graduated with a GPA of 2.52, I graduated with a GPA of 2.47 and my son graduated with a GPA of 2.11. I have found this same genetic formula to be true in all of my friends who also have family members with ADD, which is most dominant in males (but not exclusive to males).

I talked to my father about what I knew about ADD and how it impacted our grades in school. He empathized and shared with me that he was also embarrassed by his grades and struggled in most of the "memory" classes. Turns out, my father, my son and I all had similar journeys in school and in life. The school years were challenging, frustrating and embarrassing, yet once we got into the real world, life became a very fun and exciting journey. We have all done very well in life and have finally seen the gifts of ADD.

There are people with C's in school who did not try, did not show up and did not care about their grades. This book is not about them. This book is about people who gave it their best and wanted to do well. This is for those people who felt smart, but kept getting C's and D's in school. For those who kept getting told "You don't apply yourself," yet you knew you were giving it everything you had. However, with that said, there are also students who get good grades in school, who can also be ADD, or have the symptoms associated with it, so the grades are not the only indicator of someone struggling with ADD.

This book is written for those with ADD, siblings of those with ADD, the parents of those with ADD, the grandparents of those with ADD, the significant others of those with ADD and even employers of those with

ADD. It is important that everyone understand the challenges and gifts that come along with the diagnosis, because there are both. The biggest obstacle that comes with ADD is the lack of knowledge and understanding about it. Most of the people who have it don't even know they have it. And those who have been diagnosed feel isolated, like they are the only ones who struggle with it, sometimes creating self-worth issues.

People with ADD do not need pity or sympathy, but there may be situations that require patience, compassion, empathy, coaching or even medication. They need support and encouragement in their school years, and to not be berated because they are not "A" and "B" students. They need someone to point out the times when they excel or have done well. They need positive feedback about their creative or artistic side, or how their fearlessness will serve them well in life. It is easy to find the faults with ADD, but I would encourage parents to also look at the positive attributes from this gift, which can sometimes be overlooked. My hope is that this book will help enlighten and educate everyone to the struggles with ADD and the many gifts that can come along with it as well.

Not everyone is going to find the gift in ADD, especially when they are young and being judged by a traditional public education system that rewards memory, not creativity and ingenuity. ADD is like eyesight or hearing – there are many varying degrees of it and the journey is different for everyone. Especially for those who struggle in school because ADD may feel like a huge burden that intrudes on your life and makes you feel like you are separated from the herd. You might struggle and be so caught up in the emotional turmoil or the fight for good grades that you don't see the gifts.

To add insult to injury, some research has shown that many people with ADD may also have co-existing conditions such as anxiety, depression, conduct disorder, Asperger's, dyslexia, Tourette's or bipolar disorder. These can be very serious and would certainly make it difficult to see any gift from ADD. In combination, they can make your life miserable, which may explain why some of you reading this book have never been able to find the gift of ADD. Your misery and struggle may be related to the co-existing conditions and not necessarily from the ADD itself. The co-existing conditions may be "relational" but not necessarily "causational," meaning that ADD might not have caused the co-existing conditions, but they may be related (there may be correlations between them). The reason I am able to state that I have been able to embrace the gifts associated with ADD is because that is all I am dealing with – I have no related medical or psychological conditions that are compounding my ADD. I guess you could say that I am pure ADD (if there is such a thing – if not, I just invented it).

Parents of children with ADD may be especially prone to their feelings of "*What did I do wrong?*" or "*Why is my child not getting better grades?*" and taking the low grades or sometimes disruptive behavior as a personal affront to their parenting skills. It may even get more frustrating when they find out that there is no test that can be taken to absolutely confirm that their child has ADD. The diagnosis will come as a result of having teachers complete a survey about their observations of their child. It would be very easy for a teacher to declare your child disruptive or troubled based on their experiences, which might lead to a doctor's misdiagnosis. I think some children get misdiagnosed with ADD because they are simply acting like "kids."

Parents may also get frustrated when they find out that there is no cure and there is no "one size fits all" solution for everyone. Taking medication is not always the answer, so the journey can sometimes feel long and confusing. These are the times when the gift may be hard to see through the fog of frustration.

If you are truly ADD, you will probably struggle with trying to read and remember this book. Your mind will wander, you will forget where you left off or you will simply get distracted by something more fun to do. People do not fail as much as systems do, so make sure you have some good systems in place to help you remember what you are reading. For me, having a colored highlight pen to mark the content that was interesting to me is critical. Then after I read the book and highlight the important points, I will go back and re-read the highlighted points and make notes as to what action plan I will take with what I have learned.

As you are reading this book, if your brain says *"I know that"* about a particular issue, then ask yourself *"Do I do that?"* What you know is not as important as what you do with it. Many people are voracious readers and learners, but knowledge is meaningless unless you apply what you have learned. When you finish this book, I hope that you are not just inspired with the idea that ADD can provide many gifts, but that you create a plan of action for what you are going to do with your gifts. You are unique, so use your gifts to enhance your life and maybe even our world.

I truly believe there are many gifts to ADD for many people. However, this book is about my journey and the gifts that I have unearthed. It may not be your journey, your story or your experience. I am hoping that many people will be able to relate to my story, and since ADD is hereditary, they can help their children through their journey. I just hope that the frustrations that can occur in the school years do not overshadow the gifts that lie below the surface. It is very easy to be so caught up in the negatives of the diagnosis that we forget to see the positive attributes. When I was in school, I got real tired of hearing teachers tell me; *"You don't apply yourself."* I wish someone would have said, *"What feels like a struggle today, will evolve into many gifts that will serve you well in life."*

Chapter 2

I Have What?

There used to be two separate diagnoses; one was ADD (Attention Deficit Disorder) and the other was ADHD (which is Attention Deficit Hyperactivity Disorder). They were both very similar except one of the symptoms of ADHD was the hyperactivity that can occur in some children. Being fidgety and moving constantly are some of the recognizable symptoms. Today the mental health community has combined both into one diagnosis, which is AD/HD. However, you will still see all three of the diagnostic labels of ADD (the most common), ADHD and AD/HD used by many sources since there is a lack of consistent dialogue at this point.

The Encarta Dictionary defines each as:

- **Attention**: *Concentration, mental focus*
- **Deficit**: *Shortfall, lacking*
- **Hyperactivity**: *Abnormally active, restless*
- **Disorder**: *Not functioning normally*

There are currently three different types of AD/HD:

- **Inattentive AD/HD**: Involves a lack of attention (used to be ADD)

- **Hyperactive-Impulse AD/HD**: Involves hyperactivity with attentiveness
- **Combined AD/HD**: Involves all the symptoms

I believe the word "Disorder" should be banished from the entire AD/HD diagnosis, because it has the implications of being broken or not whole, which is not good for a person's self-image. If you read the full definition in the dictionary of the word "Disorder" as it relates to the medical world, it says; "*ILLNESS. A medical condition involving a disturbance to the normal functioning of the mind or body.*" The word "Disorder" can lead people with the diagnosis to possible self-sabotage through victimization or a loss of personal power by feeling they are not as capable as others. As a person with AD/HD, I don't feel "disturbed." Quite the opposite, I actually feel like my mind and body perform at a very high level.

Susan Smalley, one of the authors of a University of Los Angeles, School of Medicine Study on 120/240 polymorphism and AD/HD, said that "*calling AD/HD a "disorder" is probably not the right word. Many of these children are extremely talented. As they grow older, some find that AD/HD traits are an asset in the working world. What prevents a young boy from sitting still and concentrating in a classroom may enable him to process many things simultaneously later in life.*"

I am not disputing or denying that people with AD/HD might have brains that function differently (differently ordered), but does it have to be labeled a "disorder"? The word only serves to make people with the diagnosis feel less than other people, when they may be just as smart, and maybe even smarter (which I will talk about further in the book). I can best relate it to people who are sometimes referred to as "disabled," but the people who are affected by their difference would prefer to be called "differently-abled" in many cases. I believe that the medical community should pay more attention to the radial impact of their labeling decisions and take into consideration the long-term ramifications of the mental health impact on our children's self-image.

Most experts will tell you that AD/HD is more of an "Executive Function" difference. Executive functioning could be defined as the brains ability to organize and manage information (which happens in the Pre-frontal cortex of the brain). Unfortunately for children, school puts the highest demands on this function; which is why most children with AD/HD struggle in school and sometimes seem disorganized. Maybe the whole thing is an "Executive Function Deficit."

You could also make a point that the word "Deficit" has negative meaning as well, however, I am not as concerned with that word. If you are AD/HD, you pretty much already know you have a lack of attention. Even the word "Hyperactivity" can be considered negative by some because it is defined as abnormally active, but the word "Disorder" concerns me the most and just needs to go away.

If a person has an attention challenge, then diagnose them with Attention Deficit (AD). If a person is hyperactive, then diagnose them with Hyperactivity (H). If they have both symptoms of Attention Deficit and Hyperactivity, then diagnose them with AD/H (Attention Deficit with Hyperactivity). It just seems to make more sense and it keeps people emotionally safe from the word "Disorder" (matter of fact, I feel disordered just writing the word). So, through the rest of this book, I am no longer going to recognize the word "disorder" just out of principle. I will be using what I consider to be the proper acronym, which is AD/H. Remember; someone has to have the courage to make change, and who better than a person with creativity, ingenuity and fearlessness (someone like me with AD)?

Attention Deficit has been defined as the lack of attention (inattention). The lack of attention can sometimes be caused by a lack of interest. Maybe AD/H is truly an "Interest Deficit." As an example, if a student is not engaged in the subject matter of the class and has no interest in it, their attention may be drawn away to things that interest them more. Many children use daydreaming to escape the boredom of classes or situations they perceive as unnecessary or difficult (or the subject is so easy for them, that the class bores them). A lack of attention can result in the lack of retention, which is why people with AD/H do not typically test well. If you cannot retain what is being taught, then you cannot recall it upon command when asked to take a test on the subject.

The biggest challenge with AD/H is trying to diagnose it because there is no test at this point that can quantify its existence with absolute certainty. With most medical conditions, you can do urine or blood tests, or some other type of test that will confirm the existence of a condition. AD/H is simply observational, which leaves a lot of room for error, because it is all about perception.

Matter of fact, there is some interesting research that was done by an economist, Todd Elder, in the Journal of Health Economics (Elder et al. The importance of relative standards in AD/HD diagnoses: Evidence based on exact birth dates. Journal of Health Economics, 2010; DOI: 10.1016/j.jhealeco.2010.06.003). Elder found that the youngest, or often the most immature children, are misdiagnosed with the AD/HD label simply because of their age and exhibited maturity.

Elder also found that these younger children are significantly more likely than their older classmates to be prescribed medications like Ritalin to control their behavior. Using a sample of 12,000 children, Elder examined the difference in AD/HD diagnosis and medication rates between the youngest and oldest children in a grade. He found that the youngest kindergartners were 60 percent more likely to be diagnosed with ADHD than the oldest kindergarten children. Elder concludes that about 20 percent have likely been misdiagnosed.

"If a child is behaving poorly, if he's inattentive, if he can't sit still, it may simply be because he's 5 and the other kids are 6," said Elder. *"There's a big difference between a 5-year-old and a 6-year-old, and teachers and medical practitioners need to take that into account when evaluating whether children have AD/HD."* AD/HD has no pathology, no biological marker in the brain that clearly demonstrates its existence. Thus, its diagnosis is always subjective. While teachers are not permitted to make this diagnosis, their perceptions and opinions serve as the initial step to a diagnosis made by a doctor.

The human mind is amazing for so many reasons, but one of those is its ability to protect us from pain. As an example, if you put your hand on a hot burner, your hand will send a message to the brain through Neurons (nerve cells) that says "this is hot" and the brain reacts by sending a message back to the hand to "stop the pain," and then you remove it from the burner. So if you are a child sitting in a class, and you are either bored or struggling in the class, your brain will try to stop the pain by taking you away to a happier place. A place that brings you joy or puts you in a place where you are successful, such as daydreaming about sports, music, art, dancing, video games or other passions at which you excel. You can see the teacher and hear their voice, so you believe you are still listening, but you aren't. There is a big difference between hearing (you are passively aware of sound) and listening (you are actively focused on the sound). Listening means you are paying attention, which means you are retaining the information.

Part of the problem with your ability to learn and retain information is physical and hereditary. It is because of something called the Reticular Activating System, and most people are unaware it even exists. I speak all over the world and have been asking my audiences for 23 years if they know what the Reticular Activating System is, and 99.5 percent of the attendees have no idea that it exists. The Reticular Activating System does not just impact only a few people; it controls and dominates every one of us, but certainly in different ways and on different levels.

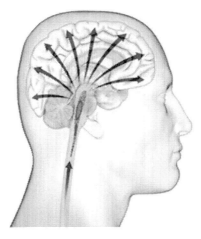

Inbound information flows through the Reticular Activating System (located inside the brain stem and mid-brain) and into other areas of the brain.

The Reticular Activating System plays a significant role in determining whether a person can learn and remember well or not and also whether they are highly motivated or bored easily. It is a loose network of neurons and neural fiber that is connected at its base to the spinal cord and runs up through the brain stem to the mid-brain. It is the center of control for other parts of the brain involved in learning, self-control or inhibitions and motivation. In short, it is the attention center of the brain, and it is the switch that turns your brain on and off. When functioning properly, it provides the connections that are needed for the processing and learning of information, plus the ability to stay focused on the correct task.

If the Reticular Activating System doesn't stimulate the neurons of the brain as much as it should, that is when people have difficulty learning, poor memory, lack of attention or self-control. If the Reticular Activating System over-stimulates the brain, then that is when people become hyperactive, talk too much and become too restless. The Reticular Activating System must be activated to normal levels for the rest of the brain to function as it should. That is why many people with AD/H are prescribed Ritalin and other such stimulant medications because it helps control the amount of stimulation to the brain.

The Reticular Activating System is best known as a filter because it sorts out what is important information that needs to be paid attention to and what is unimportant and can be ignored. Without this filter, we would all be over stimulated and distracted by noises from our environment around us. As an example, let's just say you were a mother who has a baby sleeping in the next room, and you live right next to a busy airport with lots of loud noise from jets taking off and landing. Despite the constant roar of the jets and other noise, you will hear your baby if it makes even the smallest sound in the next room. The Reticular Activating System filters out the airport noise, which is unimportant to you and keeps you focused on your baby, which is the "most important" thing to you.

Another example might be if you bought a new car, and it was a white Hyundai Sonata, all of a sudden you are noticing every white

Hyundai Sonata that passes you on the road. Your attention is heightened to something that a week earlier you would have not paid attention to. The Reticular Activating System is like a filter between your conscious mind and your subconscious mind. It takes instructions from your conscious mind (like "*I need to hear my baby*") and passes it on to your subconscious mind, which becomes diligent and alert to your request.

In the world of learning, the Reticular Activating System can act like a switch in your head that turns on and off based on how much telling-tension or self-talk you have going on inside your head. If the switch is open, you can retain information easily, and if the switch is closed, you cannot. If you are sitting in a seminar bored because the person speaking is not engaging enough (your brain is not stimulated enough), your Reticular Activating System will turn off and treat the person as irritating background noise, just like the noisy airport in a previous example. We will still see the person speaking and hear their voice, but we will not retain the information. We "hear" them, but we are not "listening" to them as described earlier.

I truly believe that if tested, we would find that many of the people with a GPA under 2.70 have some level of AD/H that is impeding their ability to do well in school, which is tied to the Reticular Activating System. In other words, I think many people with AD/H are very smart, but they probably don't test well because they cannot retain information and recall it upon command during tests (due to their Reticular Activating System).

The ability to retain information has very little to do with how smart you are; it simply means you were a member of the lucky sperm club. If you look at people who did really well in school and had great grades, you can be almost certain that at least one of their parents did as well, if not both. I know people who never studied, yet they got straight A's and in most cases, it was true of their parents as well. Those people have the gift of genealogy passed down through the family chain and their gift is a great Reticular Activating System that allows the free flow and retention of information. You cannot change your gene pool at this point because you have what you have, but you can choose how you handle what you have by knowing more about the brain and how it works.

People with a 4.0 GPA are not guaranteed to be successful in life, either in their personal life or the business world. It certainly gets them in doors and provides a great opportunity for success, but your grade point does not determine your future – you do! Your grades are not who you are, they are what the education system gave you based on what they believe "smart" is (and I believe they are wrong). AD/H is not who you are, it is what you have. Do not let others define you – you are a perfect you. Just because the world has not figured out how to score and quantify your intelligence yet, does not mean you are not going to have an extraordinary career and life.

Fifty years from now, the world will look back and see that those of us who were gifted with AD/H were the ones that changed the world for the better. We were the ones who came up with creative ideas for technology, innovation and change that made everyone's lives richer (then we hired 4.0 GPA students to work for us ☺). We will be heralded as the true visionaries and the leaders who saved the planet.

Some of the "inattention" symptoms or traits of people with AD (Attention Deficit) are:

- Low grades
- Easily bored
- Not listening
- Forgetfulness
- Lack of focus
- Procrastination
- Disorganization
- Easily distracted
- Seeming forgetful
- Short attention span
- Not keeping on task

- Avoiding mundane tasks
- Making careless mistakes
- Frequently lost in thought
- Lacking attention to details
- Lack of short term memory recall
- Not understanding directions or instructions
- The "Narrator" in your head talks constantly

Some of the "hyperactivity" symptoms or traits of people with AD/H (Attention Deficit w/Hyperactivity) are:

- Fidgeting
- Squirming
- Impatience
- Interrupting
- Walking in circles
- Talking excessively
- Wanting to make noise
- Desire to stand when seated
- Bumping into people or objects
- Starting multiple tasks & finishing none
- Trouble with quiet tasks such as reading
- Blurting out comments at an inappropriate time
- Sometimes physical activity at inappropriate times (jumping, climbing, running)

Just because you or your child exhibit a few of the above symptoms, does not mean you are AD/H, because children without AD/H can also exhibit some of the above. Adults, however, may have grown out of most of the above "hyperactivity" symptoms. If you (the adult) or your child, exhibit multiple symptoms above for at least a six month period, AD/H might be considered as a possibility. Most of the above symptoms of hyperactivity are impulsive and happen at a subconscious level. The child or adult is not giving any thought to their actions, they are simply responding to the impulse.

As a parent, it is important to know that your child is not doing the above things to make you mad or be intentionally disruptive. It is simply an impulsive reaction that they are responding to, without giving it any thought at all. Sometimes they just need to get out and run to burn the energy off. When talking to your child about specific disruptive behaviors, try to focus on the behavior or issue that you want corrected, not the child themselves. Imagine your child holding the "issue" in their hand, which is outstretched away from their body (imagine that the child and the issue are removed from each other). Talk about the issue and not the child, so that the child does not feel personally attacked by the message (so they feel emotionally safe). Let the child know they are great, but you would like the behavior or issue to improve. Just don't ask them to change things that they have no control over, which may be their hyperactivity. Their hyperactivity may need medication, coaching, counseling or some other tool to help them cope better and make them successful. Remember, if your child is hyperactive, it is more than likely your child is not intentionally being disruptive – it is impulsive and out of their control.

Possible Treatment/Solution Options:

Medications may reduce symptoms such as hyperactivity, impulsivity or poor focus. However, even though a specific medication may reduce one symptom, such as hyperactivity, it may not improve focus, so sometimes multiple medications may be prescribed because of that. The following are considered stimulant medications, but despite their name, they can sometimes provide a calming effect. They are designed to stimulate the under-active parts of the brain in people with AD/H in an effort to get them active again. In order to increase success with medications, it requires finding the right medication for your symptoms, in the right dose; taken at the right time (consistency is important). Medications may come in different forms such as pills, capsules, liquids and skin patches. These medications should never be taken without being prescribed by a medical professional.

- Ritalin (methylphenidate)
- Concerta (methylphenidate)
- Daytrana (methylphenidate)
- Metadate (methylphenidate)
- Vyvanse (lisdexamfetamine)
- Focalin (dexmethylphenidate)
- Adderall (dextroamphetamine)
- Dextrosat (dextroamphetamine)
- Dexedrine (dextroamphetamine)

There are some <u>non-stimulant medications</u> available as well. They may not be as effective as stimulants in some people; however, they may have fewer side effects. Once again, the side effects will vary by medication, so it is important to talk about each with your doctor. Here are just some options:

- Kapvey (clonidine)
- Intuniv (guanfacine)
- Effexor (venlafaxine)
- Strattera (atomoxetine)
- Wellbutrin (bupropion)
- Imipramine (tricyclic antidepressant)

There are also some blood pressure medications, such as Catapres (clonidine) and Tenex (guanfacine) that have shown to reduce symptoms of impulsivity and hyperactivity. If you are considering medication, based on a doctor's recommendation, just be alert for common side effects which can occur such as:

- Tics

- Anxiety
- Irritability
- Weight loss
- Appetite loss
- Slowed growth
- Disrupted sleep

Coaching: The word "Coach" is an old French word meaning, transporting people from where they are, to where they want to go. A personal coach who specializes in AD or AD/H can assist you in your efforts to find solutions for some of the more challenging attributes in dealing with AD/H. Here are some of the benefits to coaching as listed by an adult AD coach, Pete Quily, who resides in Vancouver, Canada (www.ADDCoach4u.com). These are the things a coach can assist you with:

- ❖ Realize Goals
  - Celebrate successes
  - Reduce procrastination
  - Provide course correction
  - Expand perception of options
  - Create AD-appreciative accountability
  - Support decision-making and prioritizing
  - Set up supportive environment for success
  - Putting the pieces in place that lead to success

- ❖ Develop New Skills
  - Learn to set boundaries
  - Manage conflict confidently
  - Personalize strategies and systems
  - Improve time and self-management
  - Manage impulsivity and distractibility

- Improve social and communication skills

❖ Manage Emotional State

- Reduce stress
- Control worry
- Reduce overwhelm
- Empower self-image
- Improve self-confidence
- Remove blame and shame

❖ AD Education

- Learn about your AD
- Discover personalized approaches
- Create a personal pattern of success
- Appreciate your strengths and unique gifts
- Understand the criteria for a successful strategy
- Draft a personalized owner's manual of your brain

Psychotherapy: Children with AD/H often participate in some form of psychotherapy to help manage their symptoms. This may include behavioral therapy, social skills training, direct contingency management or treatment in combination with medication. Parents may also take part in skills training to help in working with their children.

❖ **Behavioral Therapy:** As described by the National Institute of Mental Health, behavioral therapy strives to alter a child's behavior by reinforcing positive behavior and teaching the child to supervise his own actions. Therapists can help children to organize tasks, provide structure in their environment, and give understandable instructions. The goal of behavioral therapy is to modify behavior in such a way that children with AD/H learn how to control their own actions.

❖ **Social Skills Training:** Social skills training can be an important component of AD/H psychotherapy. According to the National Institute for Mental Health, therapists explain a particular social skill to children, such as sharing with others or raising their hand, and demonstrate how to engage in it appropriately. As described by Robert Weis in "Introduction to Child and Adolescent Psychology," social skills training may include role-playing of behaviors as well. For example, a therapist might demonstrate how to raise a hand in class by explaining the behavior, why and in what context it occurs and then modeling it. The therapist would then ask the child, or children in a group setting, to role-play a scenario where it was appropriate and be given feedback.

❖ **Parent Skills Training:** Therapists often work with parents to help them learn how to work with children with AD/H. The National Institute of Mental Health states that therapists may teach parents how to reward good behavior, punish negative behavior and use time-out to control a situation. Parents are also taught how best to help their children, by breaking down tasks into smaller pieces, structuring their environment so they do not become overstimulated, and engaging in positive joint activities with their child. It is critical to give consistent feedback, keep the child's schedule structured and organized and to commend them for doing well.

The above information on psychotherapy was from www.livestrong. com and written by Rachel Elizabeth who has a Master's of Science degree in clinical psychology from Loyola College, and she is pursuing her Doctorate in Psychology at Widener University.

Diet: Some believe that dietary changes can influence the symptoms of AD/H, but there is still a lot of debate about whether this is an effective solution in itself. Even though there are lots of theories about how sugar, carbs, preservatives and other food additives might be contributing to the symptoms of AD/H, as of the writing of this book, there are no conclusive studies offering firm results that I could find. However, eating a healthy well balanced diet, combined with exercise, would more than likely give you the best results. Excess in anything will probably not serve you well.

Supplements: There are also those who look at supplementing the diet of people with AD/H to improve the symptoms. There are some studies that have shown children with AD/H may have lower levels of Omega-3 fatty acids. Omega-3 fatty acids may have some health benefits for people with AD/H that could potentially minimize their symptoms. These are considered essential fatty acids, meaning that they cannot be synthesized by the human body but are vital for normal metabolism. Common sources of Omega-3 fatty acids include fish oils, algal oil, squid oil, and some plant oils such as echium oil and flaxseed oil.

Exercise: As mentioned earlier, I believe exercise should always be an important part of a daily regiment, along with a well-balanced diet. There are experts in this field who say people with AD/H get about four-hours of benefit immediately following a brisk workout. The biggest benefit is that of better mental focus and less distractibility after your workouts.

I work out every morning from 5:30 to 6:30 a.m. at a gym where I do 30 minutes of cardio, 10 minutes of stretching and 20 minutes of weights. I get into my office and start my work day about 7:30 a.m., and I have found that the most productive part of my day is up until about noon, then I start to see my normal symptoms of distractibility creeping their way into my life.

For children with AD/H, the worst thing you can do is put them into detention or time-out when they are acting hyper and being disruptive. They are not acting hyper or being disruptive to make parents mad – they probably never gave their actions that much thought. They are simply reacting subconsciously to the stimulus that their brain has requested. What they need is to exercise or to find a way to burn off that extra energy they have. Let them run, play or do something that their body is demanding, not cage them up to punish them. I believe the lack of knowledge about AD/H is one of the worst things for children who have it; most people don't know how to cope with it or how to handle circumstances that surround AD/H. A lot of poor parenting decisions are made based on a lack of information.

Technology: There are also some software applications for your computer or mobile phone that may help you with timeliness, organization and completing tasks on time. Depending on what your specific challenge is, you may find one of the following apps helpful to you:

- 30/30
- ReQall
- Evernote
- Toodledo
- Wunderlist
- Gtdagenda
- Leave Now
- SimpleTask
- StayOnTask
- Google Tasks
- Remember the Milk

There is no magic pill or one-size-fits-all solution to AD/H. It impacts everyone differently, and there is no single litmus test for quantifying the presence of AD/H. The fact that the diagnosis is left up to observations from parents, teachers, friends, and family, leaves a huge gap in the science. If it sounds very "hit or miss" from the diagnosis to the solutions; it is. If you read enough about it, you will get conflicting opinions from every corner of the world. There is even a psychiatrist in Australia on You Tube who says AD/H does not even exist – it is all made up.

Self-advocacy is very important for people with AD/H because no one can measure how you feel or your level or distractibility – only you. If a psychiatrist, coach, therapist, doctor, parent or teacher offers a treatment recommendation and you do not feel it is working (or has negative side-effects), it is up to you to speak up and let your voice be heard. Do not let other people decide your fate; listen to the experts, but stay active in the process of your health. Remember, AD/H is elusive, and it can require many attempts at finding a solution that fits you best. The process will proceed faster if you are more actively involved and self-advocating.

At this point, we may never get the medical or mental health community to agree on what causes AD/H, how to detect it, how to treat it, or how to cure it. Science does not have all the answers yet, and I am not sure we are even close.

Chapter 3

The Gifts Behind AD/H

Most of the people doing research on AD/H are psychologists, psychiatrists and medical doctors who are primarily trained on the pathology model, which is the precise study and diagnosis of disease. These researchers tend to be focused on the dysfunction (disorder) of AD/H. This may be because they are dealing with patients who are focused on the negative side-effects of the diagnosis. I doubt most of them have the time to try to find the gifts or benefits to AD/H. However, there are many professionals in the AD/H community beginning to acknowledge the benefits of the diagnosis, which thrills me.

Many people with AD/H have discovered some of its gifts. These three stand out:

- Creativity
- Ingenuity
- Fearlessness

Pete Quily, the AD coach I mentioned earlier, who resides in Vancouver, Canada (www.ADDCoach4u.com) took the time to list 151 positive characteristics of people with Attention Deficit, and he was kind enough to give me permission to share them with you:

1. Ability to find alternate paths to overcome obstacles
2. Able to take on large situations
3. Adaptive/collaborative
4. Adventurous, courageous, lives outside of boundaries
5. Always finding alternate routes to any given location.
6. Always willing to help others
7. Ambitious – you want to be everything when "you grow up"
8. Artistic
9. Attractive personality – magnetic due to high energy
10. Being able to see the big picture
11. Being able to see the patterns in the chaos.
12. Being intuitive towards others' difficulties
13. Broad focus – can see more, notice things more
14. Can create order from chaos
15. Can do many projects at once
16. Can make people feel they are heard
17. Can see the big picture
18. Can talk about several things at one time
19. Can think on their feet
20. Career variety
21. Center of attention
22. Comfortable talking in front of groups
23. Comfortable with change and chaos
24. Compassion for others and for themselves
25. Conceptualizes well
26. Confidence
27. Constantly evolving

28. Courageous
29. Creates connections easily
30. Creative
31. Creative writing
32. Creative – musical, artistic, "dramatic"
33. Good in a crisis
34. Good at customer relations
35. Dedicated
36. Detail-oriented
37. Determined to gain more control
38. Eager to make friends
39. Eager to try new things
40. Empathetic, sensitive
41. Energetic
42. Entrepreneurial
43. Excellent organizers using journals and reminders (notes etc.)
44. Flexible – changes as the situation requires
45. Fun to be around
46. Goal-oriented
47. Good at conceptualizing
48. Good at motivating self and others
49. Good at multitasking
50. Good at problem solving
51. Good at public speaking
52. Good at understanding others/mind reading – empathetic
53. Good conversationalist
54. Good delegator and good at organizing others

55. Good in emergency situations
56. Good listener
57. Good looking and aware of it
58. Good people skills
59. Good self-esteem, energetic
60. Great brain-stormer
61. Great multi-tasker
62. Great self-company
63. Great sense of humor
64. Great storyteller
65. Great with children (central figure around children)
66. Hands-on workers
67. Hard worker
68. Has friendly relations with their family
69. Has the gift of gab
70. Helpful
71. Helps others who are also in trouble
72. High energy – go, go, go
73. Humor, very healthy, quick picking up ideas
74. Hyper focus !!
75. Hypersensitive – very empathetic and good at non-verbal communications
76. Idea generator
77. Imaginative
78. Impulsive (in a good way) not afraid to act
79. Initiators
80. Intelligent
81. Intuitive

82. It's ok to not finish everything

83. Learning as much as they can to help children and others with AD/H

84. Less sleep is good (midnight to 6 am)

85. Like to talk a lot

86. Likes learning new things

87. Look at multidimensional sides to a situation

88. Lots of interests

89. Loves to cook and be creative

90. Magnetic

91. Master idea generator

92. Mentoring others/helpful

93. Mentoring people with low self-esteem

94. Modesty

95. Move on fast – never hold a grudge

96. Multitasks well

97. Never bored and rarely boring

98. Never intimidated to try new things

99. Non-linear, multi-dimensional/edge of chaos

100. Not afraid to speak mind

101. Not contained by boundaries.

102. On stage and ready

103. Optimistic

104. Outgoing

105. Passionate

106. Persistent

107. Philosophical

108. Holistic thinking

109. Playful
110. Pragmatic
111. Problem solver
112. Profound
113. Quick thinking
114. Quick witted
115. Relates to people easily
116. Resistant
117. Resourceful
118. Saves money in the short term by forgetting to file tax returns
119. See and remember details – recount them later
120. Sees the big picture
121. Socially adaptive and flexible.
122. Spontaneous
123. Stabilizer during difficult situations
124. Stable
125. Successful
126. Takes initiative
127. Tenacious
128. Theoretical
129. Think outside the box
130. Thinks 2 meters ahead of the world
131. Thinks big, dreams big
132. Thorough
133. Tolerant
134. Unconventional
135. Unlimited energy

136. Unorthodox

137. Versatile

138. Very creative, able to generate a lot of ideas

139. Very hard working to compensate – workaholic

140. Very intuitive

141. Very resourceful

142. Very successful

143. Visionary

144. Visual learner

145. Willing to explore

146. Willing to take risks

147. Willingness to help others

148. Witty

149. Won't tolerate boredom

150. Works well under pressure

151. Worldly

If you are diagnosed with AD/H, it does not mean you necessarily get all 151 of the gifts. It is simply a list of the some of the positive characteristics that may be present in people with the diagnosis. With that said, I have read the list numerous times and I can tell you that I have all 151 (lucky me – I knew I was special!).

However, it would be reckless of me to not note that there may be some negative behaviors or conditions that can accompany AD/H in some people. Even though I truly believe there are many wonderful gifts to AD/H, it is not all glitter and glory. Here are just some of the possible challenges for some people with AD/H:

- Anxiety
- Depression
- Temper fits

- Disobedience
- Sleep challenges
- Eating disorders
- Substance abuse
- High divorce rates
- Physical complaints
- Aggressive behavior
- Restless leg syndrome
- Relationship challenges
- Poor school performance
- Night terrors or nightmares
- Desire to harm self or others
- Refusal to seek solutions for AD/H
- Increased activity, fidgeting, movement
- Serious worries or anxiety about school
- Low grades on tests, even though they studied

Remember, many people with AD/H may have co-existing conditions such as anxiety, depression, conduct disorder, Asperger's, Tourette's or bipolar disorder. This does not mean that AD/H causes these co-existing conditions, it simply means a person may be diagnosed with both at the same time. However, with that said, I can see how a person with a low self-image, based on getting poor grades in school, could become depressed. If you are told throughout your school years that your grades are "not good enough," and it gets quantified every time your report cards come out, it would stand to reason that it could kill your self-confidence, which could lead to depression.

There have been cases where people have been taking antidepressants for their diagnoses of depression, which were made by medical doctors. When the depression did not go away, they were examined by a psychiatrist and diagnosed with AD/H. They were removed from the antidepressants and given stimulant medication to treat the AD/H. The depression went away; focus, organization, clear thinking and confidence were restored, and they became fully functioning again.

There is some research that shows people with AD/H can also have higher levels of addiction, unemployment (or under-employment), divorce, trips to jail, emergency room visits, eating disorders or suicide attempts. But once again, I question whether it is the AD/H itself causing these issues, or a low self-image that is the root cause behind them? That is why AD/H is a very complex condition with many symptoms (good and bad) and why it is difficult to generalize about people with AD/H.

That is also why I have been very careful to fully disclose that not everyone is going to feel like AD/H is a gift; because for many, it can feel more like a curse. Even though in my school years, I found the symptoms to be frustrating and an inconvenience, I never did suffer from most of the serious negative effects listed above. If you exhibit characteristics that are clearly unhealthy, please call your doctor or other health care professional and seek assistance. There are solutions; you just need to be willing to self-advocate and seek them out.

Here is a creative thought (after all, that's what those of us with AD/H excel at): Is it possible that I and many of the other people who are AD/H are the normal ones? Why is it that we have the supposed "disorder?" After all, we are the ones who are gifted with creativity, ingenuity and fearlessness. Maybe we are the ones who are actually of higher intelligence. Is it possible that people who are the stereotypical 4.0 GPA students are the ones who actually have a disorder?

It should stand to reason that if the mental health community views a "deficit" in something, such as "attention deficit" (a lack of attention) as a disorder, then there is reason to believe that people with 4.0 GPAs may also have disorders that we should be concerned about.

Possible Disorders for People with High GPAs (Grade Point Averages):

CD = Creativity Disorder (Creativity Deficit)

ID = Ingenuity Disorder (Ingenuity Deficit)

FD = Fearlessness Disorder (Fearlessness Deficit)

If people with an Attention Deficit, who are also Hyperactive, can be labeled AD/HD by the mental health community, then it would stand to reason that people with a deficit of Creativity, Ingenuity and Fearlessness should be labeled with a diagnosis like CIFD (Creativity, Ingenuity and Fearlessness Disorder).

If you think about the stereotypical brainiac (aka. stereotypical 4.0 GPA adult), they are often perceived as shy, socially awkward, having photographic memories, analytical minds, academic over-achievers and sometimes naïve (oh, and don't forget the pocket protectors because they are a dead giveaway). This group of adults tends to be traditionally deficit in creativity, ingenuity and fearlessness. They are also not much fun at parties, but we can't disorder them for that. If you want a good solid visual, watch the television show "Big Bang Theory" (which I really enjoy by the way).

Think about it; these poor stereotypical 4.0 GPA souls who have been heralded as the best and the brightest are actually all screwed up. They are a mess, and no one has told them about their disorder. What a horrible injustice that the valedictorians of the education system are actually the ones who we should be reaching out to and helping with their disorder. Which brings the question to mind; what kind of medications shall we use to drug these people, so we can help get them normal? Everyone seems to want us drugged up, so what about them and their disorder?

Without doing a lot of research on the subject, I am just going to have to shoot from the hip on this one in order to get assistance to this broken part of the population as fast as possible. If we want to increase their creativity, ingenuity and fearlessness then we need to give serious thought as to what medication might help this horrific disorder. I have it! Pot! Yes, Marijuana, Cannabis, Hemp, Hooch, Weed, Grass, Reefer, Rope, Ganga, Bud, Joint, Mary Jane, Sweet Lucy or whatever you want to call it. This would more than likely open their minds and free them from their "inside the box" thinking and their trapped perspectives that are impeding their careers and social lives.

Since Marijuana is now legal in Washington State as of 2013, all 4.0 GPA adults can move here and seek the medical assistance they need to live a more creative, ingenious and fearless life. We can open up 4.0 GPA communes or retreats where they can flock and be with their own people. It would help them cope with their disorder and find kinship with their broken brethren who are all seeking a more fulfilled life. Oh sure there may be some possible side-effects to their treatment, like cotton mouth, munchies, slow driving, the lack of desire to leave the couch for hours at a time and the overuse of the word "dude." However, it is far better than the crappy drugs we AD/H people are prescribed with potential side-effects such as:

- Nausea
- Dizziness
- Addiction
- Headache
- Depression
- Stomach ache
- Cocaine craving
- Heart palpitations
- Decreased appetite
- High blood pressure
- Urinary tract infection
- Infection or viral infection
- Trouble sleeping (insomnia)
- Eyesight changes or blurred vision
- Feelings of suspicion and paranoia
- Dermatoses (infected or diseased skin)
- Tolerance (constant need to raise the dose)
- Rapid pulse rate (and other heart problems)
- Slowing of growth (height and weight) in children

- Seizures, mainly in patients with a history of seizures
- Visual hallucinations (seeing things that are not there)
- Nervousness including agitation, anxiety and irritability
- Elevated ALT enzyme levels in the blood (signaling liver damage)

Who got the crappy end of the drug deal on that one? We did! Oh, and it gets worse, if you overdose on your AD/H medications, here are some of the symptoms you might experience:

- Tremor
- Sweating
- Vomiting
- Delusions
- Aggression
- Panic states
- Restlessness
- Dehydration
- Hyperreflexia
- Hallucinations
- Rapid heart beat
- Personality changes
- High blood pressure
- Lower abdominal pain
- Symptoms of depression
- Unexplained muscle pain
- Seizures or abnormal EEGs
- Swelling of hands/feet/ankles
- Rhabdomyolysis and kidney damage

- Chronic abuse can manifest itself as psychosis, often indistinguishable from schizophrenia

If the 4.0 GPA people, who have CIFD (Creativity, Ingenuity and Fearlessness Disorder), overdose on their Marijuana medication, the symptoms are:

- Fall asleep on couch

Oh my god, call 911!

Heck, you just give them a pillow and bottle of water for when they wake up with cotton mouth, and they will be fine.

As you may have noticed by now, much of this chapter was laced with sarcasm and humor (I am not very good at hiding it), but it was to make a point. In all seriousness, I am not trying to minimize the scholastic achievements of people who get good grades because most of them work very hard to achieve such results. I intentionally used the word "stereotypical" because everyone is very unique and cannot be put into classes or groups easily. The same can be said about people with AD/H because there are also the stereotypes about people with that diagnosis, which if flavored with some humor, can actually be very funny (I laugh at myself all the time).

My attack is not on 4.0 GPA students or their scholastic achievements, because some of them are also AD/H; it is on the traditional public education system. I believe it is antiquated in its method of measuring "smart." I challenge anyone or any system that labels me and my 2.47 GPA as any less "smart" than most of the kids I graduated with from high school who had GPAs of 3.5 or 4.0. I challenge the thought that the ability to retain and recall information upon demand is "smart" – they simply have the gift of retention and regurgitation.

All of us have special gifts; they are not all the same. They will never be the same and more importantly, they shouldn't be the same. People with a 4.0 GPA have an amazing gift of retention and recall – they have great memories. It is a very unique gift that only about 3 percent of the population has; so congratulations if you are one of the lucky few. Your gifts and talents are sorely needed in this world and you will find a job duty in the workplace that fits your gifts perfectly. You will love your job because you are good at your craft – the perfect position for your gift. This helps build your confidence, which serves you well in both your career and personal life.

Many people with AD/H, who have GPAs like me (2.47), have special gifts as well, such as creativity, ingenuity and fearlessness. They are very unique gifts, so we too should be celebrated because the world needs our gifts. There are very few businesses that could survive without our gifts, so they are lucky to have us. Because of our unique gifts, we are also the creators of jobs. We are the fearless entrepreneurs who create companies and hire people to help us build them. We hire 2.47 GPA people for sales, advertising, marketing, public relations and other jobs suited to our gifts. We also hire 4.0 GPA people to become our bookkeepers, operations managers, network administrators, computer programmers or research and development. These people are perfectly suited for those jobs because of their unique gifts. If you are doing a job that you are good at, it helps build your self-confidence, which has a dramatic impact on both your business and personal lives.

The way the grading system is designed today in most public schools, it celebrates 4.0 GPA gifts and not the gifts that the rest of us possess. It holds up a tiny part of the population and says "*This is what we want you all to aspire to*" (good retention and recall), which is never going to happen under the current system. It is actually physically impossible today, which means the current system is created for many of us to fail. We are setting close to 50 percent of our children up for failure, which will stay with them the rest of their lives. Our current grading system is designed to decimate self-confidence – the one thing that we are in short supply of in this world. How can we continue to let this happen when we know it is so wrong? If we found a disease that impacted close to 50 percent of the population, we would call it an epidemic, and put all of our resources to work to find immediate solutions. This is one of the largest and most costly epidemics of our time, and it will never even make the back page of a local newspaper.

I will cover this in more detail in an upcoming chapter titled "**The System is Broken, Not You,**" that deals with the education system. As mentioned, even 4.0 students can have AD/H and struggle with some of the same challenges that those of us with AD/H do. However, it is less common, and it is certainly easier to spot and diagnose in those of us who are stereotypical AD/H because of our hyperactivity or lower grades. The more you learn about AD/H, the more confusing it may become because you will see that there is no one exempt from the possibility of having it (race, gender, age, ethnicity, religion, sexual orientation, etc.).

If you are AD/H, I hope you discover that you actually have many of the gifts listed in this chapter. The goal of this book is to focus on the positive attributes and the possible gifts behind the diagnosis and not the negatives, which tend to get the most attention. I believe that where our thoughts go, energy flows; so if you focus on the misery behind AD/H, then you may attract more misery into your life. I try to focus on the benefits and gifts behind AD/H, and I believe the change in thought and energy has provided me with an extraordinary career and life.

I want people to feel hope and see opportunity before them. I want people to know that they are not alone and there are millions of people just like them (I believe the number is grossly underestimated by the experts). You are not dumb, even though the education system made you feel that way – you are brilliant in so many other ways. I want people to at least consider the possibility that they are not broken - maybe it is the traditional public education system that is broken. Our grades should not define us because that is not who we are, they are what the misguided education system gave us during a very short period of our life. AD/H is not who we are, it is what we have.

Chapter 4

Does Size Really Matter?

I t is certainly understandable that numbers are a valuable metric that most of us live and breathe by every day. It would be pretty unusual to make it through an entire day without having to deal with numbers, whether it is the amount of money in your checking account, the speed you are driving, the number of donuts you ordered, an address you were looking for, or your password that allows you access to Internet sites. Numbers are here to stay, so we will certainly have to get used to them.

However, many numbers become emotional wounds and confidence killers that can impact us for life. There are numbers that become the defining moment for our self-image or self-worth. There are numbers that help reinforce the voice of our inner saboteur and make it easier for it to erode our self-confidence. They are just simple everyday numbers; the kind of numbers that we dealt with in math when we were in school, but these numbers can sometimes shape our future.

You are a young man who wants to play college basketball more than anything, but you are only 5 feet 7 inches tall. You have good basketball skills, but you keep getting turned down on your applications based on someone you have never even met's perception of what makes a great player – you are not tall enough. Your skills are blindly overlooked because of some numbers that don't fit the standard profile of a successful college basketball player. Yet, people rarely look at exceptions like Spud Webb who was only 5 foot-7-inches tall, but played 13 years in the NBA, scored 8,072 points and had 4,342 assists in his career. He also won an NBA slam dunk contest in 1986. There were even two NBA players shorter than Spud, and they were Earl Boykins and Muggsy Bogues. The reality is, your height is not who you are, it is simply a vertical numeric dimension of your body.

As a child growing up, you have struggled with weight all your life and you were teased relentlessly by other children. You were judged, not by who you truly were, but by the numbers on the scale. You had a great sense of humor, showed tremendous skill as an artist, and you did well in school. But, people's perceptions of you were skewed because of numbers that blinded them to the fabulous person you truly are. Because you did not fit into the standard norms for weight, you were unfairly labeled and thrown into a category for other people's convenience. It crushed your self-worth and confidence, filling your school years with painful memories. The reality is your weight is not who you are, it is simply a numeric standard of measurement.

You are a young man who is smart, charismatic and a high school letterman in three sports that people are drawn to. Women find you attractive, so you have no problem filling up your social calendar. However, over the years, you have heard women joking and talking about how they would never date anyone who did not have at least an 8-inch penis. You are only 5 inches, so you question your value and wonder whether women laugh behind your back or if they are unsatisfied. This uncertainty creates an underlying self-image issue and insecurities based solely on a number from random social conversations. The reality is, the size of your penis is not who you are, it is simply a body part.

Women can probably also relate to similar circumstances of growing up in the 60s and 70s with a Barbie doll that had huge breasts in proportion to her actual size. You read Hollywood gossip magazines that show the young starlets having breast implants in order to further their careers. After physical education classes in school, you change clothes in the locker room and could see that your breasts were not as developed as other girls your age, so you were embarrassed to be seen without a top on. How did that shape your self-worth? How did that impact your confidence in other aspects of your life? The reality is, the size of your breasts is not who you are, it is simply a body part.

As you learned from my story about growing up with poor grades, I let my grade point average (2.47) define me and make me feel like I was not good enough. It also got reinforced once a quarter when grades came out, or when applying for a scholarship, applying to a University or applying for a job. The world looks at your number, judges you for that number and makes decisions about your life based on that number.

The same is true for much of our developmental school years with GPA, SAT, ACT, or IQ scores. They supposedly tell the world if we are worthy of greatness – it's a bunch of crap! What a horrible time of life to be labeled with random scores, right when you are trying to define yourself and are influenced so heavily by other's perceptions of you. I understand the need to quantify performance because I also believe that we must inspect what we expect out of people. If the scores were truly reflective of "smart," I might not have any problem with them. However, I still believe we are light years away from having quantitative numbers that truly define that measure.

Whether it is your family, friends or the education system talking; being told that you are "not good enough" is painful and can change your self-image for life. When it is some person's misguided opinion of you, it leaves a wound, but when the education system quantifies it for you in writing, it becomes a scar. The reality is, numbers should not define us – they are what we have, but they are not who we are.

Your GPA, SAT, ACT or IQ scores are no guarantee of success or failure. Yes, it is a great achievement when your numbers are high. Sure, it gives you a great resumé and an edge in job interviews when you first enter the job market (after that, no one will ever ask you again). I believe the most important thing it does for you when you score well, is it builds your confidence. However, high scores will not be the differentiating factor in whether you will have a great career or life. Numbers only have the meaning that we attach to them.

I believe the most important factor in success for all people is their level of confidence. That is why it pains me to see children being minimized by their grades, height, weight, body differences or anything else. Uncertainty kills dreams and uncertainty about ourselves kills confidence, which ultimately erodes our self-image. The biggest gift we can give our youth is that of feeling good about themselves – a feeling of confidence in some areas of their life. If they struggle in school today, then provide them with the opportunity to be successful at something else, whether it is sports, art, music, writing, poetry, or for whatever they find a passion.

Chapter 5

Creativity – Embrace the Narrator

Creativity is something that I am extremely grateful for. I believe it is one of the gifts I was given, that often comes along with the diagnosis of AD/H (once again, not everyone will have each gift). I have lived a life that has no boundaries because much of my thinking comes from outside of the box. "The box" I am talking about, that traps so many great ideas, is an emotional box that can stifle creativity and action. Whenever you think about wanting to "step outside the box" and take some emotional risk, you might hear a voice in your head that says *"But what if you fail?"* This voice is trying to scare you back to conformity and keep you from moving forward with your ideas and further creative thought.

Where other people see objections and restrictions to their creative thoughts, I see possibility and opportunity. Possibility and opportunity can lead you to success if you are open to it and not inhibited by fear. Matter of fact, in my seminar titled *"Simple Steps to an Extraordinary Career & Life"* I list the following formula for success:

Choice = Possibility = Opportunity = Success

Creativity is about choice and not being restricted by the idea that there is only one way to do things. People, including myself, who have the gift of creativity don't let roadblocks get in our way. We have the innate ability to think more creatively (outside the box) and come up with solutions instead of getting side-tracked by the problems. Once you learn through creativity that there is choice to almost everything, it opens up possibilities you may not have seen before. Once you can envision possibility, you can see what opportunities lie ahead of you, and from there, success is right around the corner.

People with AD/H tend to have the gift of "**divergent**" thinking (out of the box thinking), which is the brain's ability to produce spontaneous, innovative and creative ideas and solutions. This gift is well suited for creative jobs like entrepreneurs, sales, marketing, graphic arts, theater, drama, etc. Many people who I have referred to as "Stereotypical 4.0 GPAs," tend to have the gift of "**convergent**" thinking (inside the box thinking), which is the brain's ability to focus on the heart of the problem, analyze the situation based on what they know and find one correct solution. This gift is well suited for accountants, scientists, medical doctors, programmers, etc. Neither is right or wrong – we need both in this world for all of us to survive and be successful. They both need to be celebrated!

There was actually some research done on AD/H and the gift of creativity. Holly A. White from the University of Memphis and Priti Shah from the University of Michigan published an AD/H and creativity study, which indicated adults with AD/H showed higher levels of original creative thinking and higher levels of real-world creative achievement, compared to adults without AD/H. This study was published in the Journal of Personality and Individual Differences (January 2011). They found that when faced with a problem, most people would prefer to refine and clarify ideas, whereas, people with AD/H focused more on generating new and innovative ideas (brainstorming). This new study supports their earlier 2006 research. According to White, a distinct pattern emerged: AD/H subjects were more likely to excel at certain creative domains than at others – especially the performing arts.

Domains where inhibition is not necessary seem to be the areas where these students excel, especially in theater and drama.

Are people with AD/H also more positive thinkers and more optimistic than others? I can't quantify that, however, I believe it to be true. I have always been a positive thinker, and like Zig Ziglar once said *"An optimist is someone who goes after Moby Dick in a row boat and takes the tarter-sauce with them!"* I believe optimism is one of the great attributes of successful entrepreneurs.

When it comes to creativity, my brain is always alert and analyzing the world around me – it is looking for a "better way." As an example, if I am driving up to a shopping mall, my creative mind will see that a tree has grown up in front of the sign, blocking its visibility. I wonder why the mall management hasn't noticed it and cut it down to increase customer visibility. As I look for a place to park, I wonder why they put in so many planters, which reduced valuable parking spaces by at least 10 percent, stressing customers trying to find spots to park. As I enter through the malls main doors, I notice that the entry floor is tile, and when wet, is slippery, which might cause someone to fall, which is a horrible liability for the mall.

As I am walking through the shopping mall, I will notice a sign advertising children's socks at half price, but it is hanging too high where women and children cannot see it. I look into the store and see four employees standing around the cash stand talking socially when they should be folding clothes that customers have messed up, or approaching customers who might need assistance. I also wonder where the manager is and why they allow that kind of behavior from the employees. I will notice that 10 percent of the lights in the mall are not working, and wonder if anyone even knows about it, or cares that it reflects poorly on the brand of the mall.

I have a narrator in my head that is working full time, to broadcast curious and creative thoughts to me as I move throughout the day. It is even doing it right now as I write this book – speaking to me and providing me with creative dialogue. The narrator in my head might drive a weaker person to insanity because the darn voice never shuts up. It is relentless in its pursuit to enlighten and educate me to how the world could be a better place and how businesses could be more successful. I am always thinking about the next seminar, the next book, the next service I can offer, the next company I might start or the next great undiscovered idea to replace the Shamwow or Snuggie. Yes, it can be exhausting.

Dr. Edward Hallowell, is a very well respected child and adult psychiatrist, NY Times bestselling author and leading authority in the field of AD/HD. He had a fabulous analogy when trying to describe to children what AD/HD is. He tells children they have a race-car brain with bicycle brakes. Their brains are like a Ferrari – very fast – but they need help controlling it sometimes. Dr. Hallowell and his sons are also AD/H, so he comes from a place of empathy and understands the journey of people with the diagnoses. He was one of the first experts I heard speak who agreed that there are many gifts to AD/H. When asked if he would give up his gift or want his kids not to have AD/H, he said he would not change a thing, which is exactly the way I feel. As I said before, the inner voice (or narrator) talks very fast (like a Ferrari) and can be relentless, but I would not give it up for anything. And like his analogy stated, it can be very hard to stop (with bicycle brakes), especially at the end of the day when I want to relax.

Most people with AD/H assume that everyone has a narrator in their head with persistent dialogue. We are so used to it that we do not think it is unusual or that it is unique to us. I never really realized until I was 50 years old that most people do not have that relentless voice jabbering in their head. I was shocked when I told people about my Attention Deficit, and how the narrator in my head is hard to stop at the end of the day. People would look at me like I was an alien and wonder what I was talking about. It was then that I realized that the voice in my head was unique to those of us with the gift.

I have many good friends with AD/H; some medicated and some not. When I bring up the conversation about the narrator in my head for the first time to them, they get a very inquisitive look on their face and ask "*You mean most people don't have that constant voice in their head?"* It is truly an amazing discovery for people of all ages with AD/H to learn that not everyone has a brain that active. We have all had it most of our lives, so how on earth would we know any different? It's not the kind of conversation you have with other people when you meet them: *"Hey Bob, nice to meet you – say, do you have a voice in your head too that talks non-stop?"*

I was relaxing in the spa with my wife the other morning after our early morning workout, and she saw my mind working (she can see it in my eyes) and asked me what I was thinking about. So I told her that my narrator was noticing the amount of debris in my neighbor's gutters and wondered if they knew it was there. It was questioning why the neighbor planted three "like" trees that block our view, but why one of them was a different color than the other two. It was curious as to why a construction truck was driving in our neighborhood at 6:30 in the morning. My narrator was thinking about what type of cleaner I was going to need to clean the mildew off our awning, which it just noticed. It saw small cracks in the siding to our home and questioned when those should be caulked to prevent water damage. All of that dialogue happened in less than one minute. I asked my wife what she was thinking about, and her answer was *"Nothing, absolutely nothing."* That is a good example of the difference between people with AD/H and people without.

My mind starts its creative rambling from the moment I get up until the time I go to sleep. The inner voice is a huge gift throughout the day because I have learned that the narrator is what feeds my creativity, exercises my curiosity muscle and provides me with such great ideas. The voice might sound like a pest, but I have learned to embrace this fabulous gift by paying attention to the verbal chatter, keeping an eye out for opportunity. The narrator in my head is extremely smart; so I know if I listen intently, it will guide me to greater opportunities that others may not see.

I think many people with AD/H ignore the voice or try to drown it out with music or other distractions, but I pay attention to it because I know it is trying to help me. It is advocating for me and looking to provide me with opportunity, and that is why I work in my office all day in silence. It might drive some people crazy to not have any music, talk radio, water fall or something to break the silence, but I like it quiet because it allows me to hear the narrator better (I don't want to miss anything).

However, at the end of the day when it is time to stop work, it wants to continue to talk to me. It does not seem to know the work day is done, so it rambles on like a drunken uncle deep into the evening. My wife and I have a method for winding the inner voice down at the end of the day. When she comes home from work, we sit down on the sofa for anywhere from 30 to 60 minutes and we talk. We tell each other about our day, and even vent if needed, but we download any remaining thoughts that my inner voice may be harboring. We have also added a glass of wine to our communication happy hour, which I have found to be very helpful in slowing that motor mouth down (not my wife, the narrator). It really does help me get to a relaxed state where I can stop thinking about work and recharge my batteries in preparation for the next day.

Speaking of slowing the voice down, there was a news story a few weeks ago on the television that actually talked about how medical marijuana should be legalized for people with AD/H. It stated that it can help people with AD/H focus and become more productive. It makes sense because I have known very successful entrepreneurs who were admittedly AD/H and smoked a little marijuana each day, so they could stay focused on their work (it slows the narrator down to a slow crawl). I do not use marijuana, and I am not promoting the use of it; I am simply stating some facts that recently came to light, which I found fascinating but not surprising by any means.

There are many other ways to slow the voice in your head besides medicating yourself with liquor or drugs (not the best answer by any stretch). Each person, based on their own personal interests, will find their own solutions to silencing the narrator (or at least wear it down) and here are just a few options:

- Yoga
- Sports

- Skating
- Dancing
- Running
- Bicycling
- Swimming
- Video Games
- Watch Television
- Working out (exercise)
- Meditation (sometimes challenging for those with AD/H due to the amount of focus required)

Basically, anything that diverts your attention or disengages you from normal thought, and wears you out, can be beneficial. If you can get your narrator tired, it may slow down and allow you to relax. Studies have found that engaging in physical activities not only improves physical health, but also helps in treating depression and other possible co-existing conditions that can accompany AD/H. As mentioned earlier, you can get up to four-hours of increased focus and productivity after a workout, so exercise is always going to provide great benefits.

I have also put a few systems in place to help me sleep throughout the night and keep my narrator as quiet as possible. I put a spiral notepad in my nightstand along with a pen that I stick into the spiral spine of the notebook, so I can find it in the middle of the night (the pen even has a light on it for writing in the dark). Whenever an idea pops into my head, the narrator starts replaying it over and over again, this can keep me awake. When it happens, I will quietly open my nightstand drawer, so I don't wake my wife, retrieve my notepad and write down whatever thought is rolling around in my head and then put the notepad back when I am done. This allows me to drain my brain and get back to sleep. Otherwise, I will lay there listening to the narrator and trying not to forget whatever is so important, losing hours of sleep.

People with AD/H express their creativity in many ways; through art, music, dance, cooking, writing, poetry, photography, theater, magic, film, sewing, martial arts, sculpting, architecture, pottery, animation, business and in many other ways. Here are a few of the recognizable celebrities who have, or were thought to have AD/H and the gift of creativity:

- Walt Disney
- Jim Carrey
- Ann Bancroft
- Steve McQueen
- Jack Nicholson
- Will Smith
- Whoopi Goldberg
- Woody Harrelson
- Ty Pennington
- Sylvester Stallone
- Robin Williams
- Howie Mandel
- Henry Winkler
- Stevie Wonder
- Cher
- Elvis Presley
- Curt Cobain
- Adam Levine
- Picasso
- Vincent Van Gough
- Wolfgang Amadeus Mozart
- Beethoven
- Hans Christian Anderson

- Leonardo da Vinci
- Samuel Clemens
- Emily Dickenson
- Edgar Allan Poe
- John Grisham
- Ralph Waldo Emerson
- Henry David Thoreau
- Robert Frost
- Tennessee Williams
- Virginia Woolf

Some of the people above not only have the creative side that comes along with AD/H, but they may have had to deal with co-existing disorders such as anxiety, depression, dyslexia, conduct disorder, Asperger's, Tourette's or bipolar disorder. Even though many have had very successful careers and seemed happy from an outside perspective, their personal lives may have been impacted with depression or anxiety. Many of the people on this list are also well known marijuana users, (which they may have found helpful in controlling their symptoms).

Chapter 6

Ingenuity – Building a Better Mousetrap

Many people with AD/H make great business people, entrepreneurs and leaders because they have many of the characteristics required. Here are just some of the key traits of successful entrepreneurs:

- **Smart** – not necessarily book smart – but street smart.
- **Fearless** – believing the biggest risks bring the biggest rewards.
- **Initiative** – not letting opportunity pass you by – go for it!
- **Ingenuity** – building a better mousetrap by "out of the box" thinking.
- **Creativity** – an imagination with very few boundaries.
- **Visionary** – an inventive side that sees what others don't.
- **Confidence** – in their own abilities, ideas and creations.
- **Charismatic** – a great personality to attract investors and customers.
- **Competitive** – always trying to prove that you are "good enough."
- **Perseverance** – a "can do" attitude that does not allow the words "I can't."

- **High Energy** – you are fueled by passion and you have energy to burn.

- **Good Judgment** – thinking quickly on your feet and making decisions on the fly.

- **Eye For Opportunity** – listening to the narrator and exercising your curiosity muscle.

Can people without AD/H also have some of the above characteristics? Sure they can. They are not exclusive to people with AD/H, but what I believe you will find is that most of the above characteristics reside in many people with AD/H. I believe that a startling percentage of successful entrepreneurs in this world would be diagnosed with some level of AD/H.

A person might have a great idea for a new product or business, but if you can't move it forward and execute the plan, it is useless. People with AD/H have a way of thinking against the grain (lateral thinking) and seeking solutions in unorthodox methods, which might be ignored by logical thinkers (stereotypical 4.0 GPAs). I believe that is the unique difference between people with and without AD/H. I am fortunate to possess every single one of the traits listed above, but as I mentioned earlier, I believe I am pure AD/H and do not have any co-existing conditions that muddy the waters of my gift.

How many great inventions and products sit idle in someone's mind because they are too limited in their thinking? The creator might have done very well in school, so they are book smart, but they may not be street **smart**, so they lack the ability to overcome the perceived hurdles they create in their mind. They are frozen in time waiting for someone to provide them with the answers. Many people with the gift of AD/H have **vision** that most other people do not have. They see the future, they see possibility, and in most cases, they can even see the path to success. Their minds are always active, and instead of focusing on the problems, they are seeking solutions. They not only have the innovative ideas, but they know how to execute them, which is critical to success.

Those of us with AD/H don't let opportunity pass us by. We are listening eagerly to the narrator as it looks at the world through its curious mind, and when we see opportunity, we take the **initiative** to pounce on it. We are not filling our heads with the *"but what if it doesn't work?"* or *"but what if I fail?"* scenarios. Instead, we are **fearless** as we take an idea and move it forward. The analytical minds of stereotypical book smart people will sometimes lose momentum when analysis causes paralysis, and the idea or concept dies a sudden and painful death. This is not true for people with AD/H; we are like pit-bulls, fearlessly pushing forward at breakneck speed. We are relentless in the pursuit of our dreams and visions.

If we run into a roadblock, we have the gift of **ingenuity**, so we will find a "work around" or come up with another route to our designated goal. We are not only open to new routes, ideas and ways of doing business; we embrace them and take pride in our unique abilities. We are creative and have artistic blood flowing through our veins. We know what is best for our customers and how to serve their needs. We embrace our gift of **creativity** in our approach to building, marketing and advertising our business. We are not just taking the path least traveled – we are making our own path from scratch. Why? Because we can!

We have a persona of **confidence** because we believe in our abilities, ideas and creations. We know we are smarter than our grades in school showed and we are willing to show the world what we are made of. There is a brilliance in us that is yet unrecognized and hard to quantify, but we are optimistic about our bright future. We are good with people and exhibit emotional intelligence, which is the ability to connect with people at an emotional level. We can influence people with our words, smile and intelligent conversation. We are gifted and well-spoken orators who people pay attention to. We are **charismatic** – people are drawn to us and want to follow us. These fabulous characteristics are what make us great leaders of people.

Because many of us had low grades in school, we are still trying to prove to the world that we are "good enough," so we are **competitive** and not wanting to get beat. We know what we want, have a path to get it and will show tremendous discipline and drive on the journey. We demonstrate amazing **perseverance** and "can do" attitude. Employees stand behind us and are driven by our enthusiasm and determination. They are motivated by our passion and disciples of our message; willing to follow us on our amazing journey.

Those of us with AD/H have **high energy** and seem unflappable in our quest to be successful. People are motivated by our energy and are inspired to work at the same pace as us. We possess the power of influence and have the ability to change other people's behaviors by our own actions. We can work a 12-hour day, when doing what we love to do, and need to sometimes talk ourselves into taking a break. We work from a place of passion, which feeds our souls and helps us sustain our energy throughout the day. Even though we are AD/H and sometimes struggle with focus – when we are doing something we love, we can become "hyper-focused" and stay effortlessly on task for hours at a time.

We exhibit **sound judgment** in our decision making and can make quick decisions on the fly – we are decisive. We think quickly on our feet because our minds are always active and alert to the world around us. We are intuitive and don't need reports to run our businesses; we know when things are running right. Even when we are caught up in working "in the business," we are always cognizant that working "on the business" is just as important. This means we are alert and always keeping our **eye out for opportunity**. Things might be good, but we are always open to the idea that they could be better. We are open for new opportunities and always aware of our surroundings, doing our due diligence and listening to the narrator for the next great idea.

As I mentioned earlier, my father is also AD/H and throughout my entire life I have been amazed by his creativity, ingenuity and fearless-ness (and all the other attributes listed in the first part of this chapter, which he demonstrated). Back in the early 60s, my dad had an old high school buddy who drank too much, passed out with a cigarette in his hand, caught the mattress on fire and burned to death. That is what got my dad thinking about solutions for such situations. He created a vision for having smoke detectors in every home, hotel and other businesses.

There was no such thing as a smoke detector in those days, so my dad enlisted a couple of friends to help with the creation of his vision. One person was a gentleman who just came out of the military and had an education in electronic engineering (the book smart guy). My dad painted the vision of what he wanted, the engineer carried out the design, and together they created one of the first working smoke detectors.

My dad even stepped out of his comfort zone and went to Olympia and talked to his state representative about the possibility of passing a law that would require businesses to have smoke detectors. However, the two other partners drifted away, and the product never made it to market. A few years later, the state of Washington passed a law requiring smoke detectors in hotels and motels. That is a great example of his creativity, ingenuity and fearlessness; it just did not get fully executed in this one particular case.

Besides working in a mill full time, my dad was also a gillnet fisherman (just one of the ways he exercised his entrepreneurial spirit). He bought a 30-foot fishing boat back in the early 60s and named it "BJ" (after myself and my sister Judy, but it also worked for my mom whose name is Betty Jean). He was always working on the boat, trying to make it more efficient, safer and easier to use. When he was laying out his net, he wanted a way to be able to put the boat in and out of gear faster while working from the back of the boat (he wanted a control near the stern of the boat – most controls are up forward by the cabin). However, he did not want to put a typical gear shift lever anywhere near the net because the loops of the net might catch on the lever and accidently put it into gear, which could be disastrous and possibly fatal.

He came up with the idea to eliminate the shift lever by making a control that has three buttons that would

1. Shift the boat into neutral
2. Shift the boat into forward
3. Shift the boat into reverse

He bought all the individual components he needed to create this innovative solution, and what he could not buy, he made. He bought a solenoid switch (a device consisting of a cylindrical coil of wire surrounding a movable iron core that moves along the length of the coil when an electric current is passed through it), which electrically shifted the transmission. At the time, there was no such electronic control available on the market, so he made it.

My dad's gillnet fishing boat; full of innovation

He also noticed that as he was laying his net out, some of the loose netting would fall off the reel and on to the floor of the boat before going into the water. This could cause it to get tangled on his feet or other equipment near the stern of the boat. Instead of complaining about it, Dad looked at what he could do differently in order to solve the problem. There was nothing out on the market to solve the issue, so he bought a small 1.5 horse motor and materials to make the stern roller motorized, so it would keep the net moving from the reel to the water, without falling to the floor of the boat. It worked, but he could not control the speed of the stern roller, so he replaced the electric motor with a hydraulic motor, which worked perfectly. He had an inventive solution that he executed with nothing more than his creativity and ingenuity.

Back in 1984, my dad belonged to a flying club with some friends, and they had a Cessna 170 that needed to be painted. Instead of hiring someone to do it, my dad decided that he could do it (once again, the creativity, ingenuity and fearlessness comes to life). Being resourceful, he hooked up an electric motor to a compressor he bought, and found a used metal cylinder that would work as an air tank. He used one of the diffusers from one of my mom's perfume bottles as the spray nozzle, bought an air hose and some fittings and he proceeded to paint the entire plane in gold, red and white. It looked incredible and you would have never known it was not done by a professional.

My dad and the Cessna 170 he painted in 1984

I truly have hundreds of examples of my dad's creativity, ingenuity and fearlessness, which I now look back on and realize were the gifts of AD/H. I always wanted to be just like my dad because he was like the MacGyver (from the TV show called "MacGyver" that aired from 1985 to 1992) of his time. Give him a paperclip and string, and I believe he could build a chairlift for a ski area. His ingenuity and creativity are truly gifts that not everyone has.

Some of my close friends refer to me as "MacGyver," which I am very proud of because I am just like my dad; creative, ingenious and fearless. Yet, my father, my son and I were given grades in school that reprimanded us for not being smart enough (according to the education systems measure of "smart"). All three generations of Worthley boys came away from school with low self-worth and self-image issues that will be with us the rest of our lives. Even though we all know better, and we believe we are very smart, the emotional wounds live on. However, each of us has shown the world that we are capable of greatness, and we are all very smart. Will the education system update our records for our achievements and apologize for berating us with the statement, "*You don't apply yourself*"? Will we be given emotional reparation from the education system for their irresponsible labels and unfair treatment? I will wait patiently with my face pressed against the mailbox for that letter to arrive (boy, that is going to leave a mark ☺).

Here are a few of the recognizable celebrities who have or were thought to have AD/H and the gift of ingenuity. The interesting thing about AD/H, is that many people who are considered geniuses and have demonstrated incredible intelligence beyond most other people, show many of the symptoms of AD/H (Coincidence? I don't think so!):

- Frank Lloyd Wright
- Bill Gates
- Steve Jobs
- Alexander Graham Bell
- Thomas Edison
- Benjamin Franklin
- Albert Einstein
- Wright Brothers
- Richard Branson
- Ted Turner
- Malcolm Forbes

- Andrew Carnegie
- David Neeleman (Jet Blue Airline Founder)
- Paul Orfalea (Kinkos Founder)
- Henry Ford
- James Carville

Chapter 7

Fearlessness – Get Out of My Way!

As I look back at my life, I see a fearlessness that most people did not have. I have loved taking risks as far back as I can remember. Not necessarily reckless or irresponsible risk, but risk based on the potential for success based on my own perceived athletic skills, (which is obviously very subjective). I think it was harder on my parents as they watched my fearlessness unfold over my life. To them, many of the things I did may have seemed reckless or beyond the boundaries of sanity; but to me, they were all executable and worth attempting.

It's certainly one of the challenges to being a parent to someone like me with AD/H. You see unbridled energy that you can't contain when you think it should be contained. You can't understand why your child won't just sit still and "act like other children." You are frustrated when they don't seem to pay attention when you are talking or giving them directions. You see them climbing tall trees, knowing that if they fell, they would break their necks. They build large ramps out of scrap wood from the garage off which to jump their bicycles, which seems like a really bad idea to you. Their curiosity sends them into the woods exploring where their chance of getting lost is very high. Your child wants to jump off the top of the play set in the backyard with an open umbrella, just to see what would happen.

As a parent, this fearlessness is terrifying and you want to protect your children from harm. Some of their ideas are just plain stupid and you know that it's just a matter of time before they injure themselves. You view some of their behaviors as disruptive and a challenge to your authority. It might even cross your mind that they are behaving the way they are just to be rebellious or to intentionally make your life miserable. The more you try to reel them in and control their every move, the more you are frustrated when you fail at your mission. It is very easy to view these behaviors, and the characteristic of fearlessness, as a bad thing. However, I would like you to give consideration as to how it may serve them later in life. Will this fearlessness translate into an adult who is an inventor, a musician who creates innovative music, an artist who sees no boundaries or a successful entrepreneur who is willing to take risks and invent the future?

When I was in high school, we used to drive out to the Humptulips River, (yes, there is actually a town by that name and it's where my mother was raised) and I would dive off of the railroad bridge into the freezing river just for fun. I am guessing it was a 40-foot drop, which may not sound like much, but when you are up there looking down, it looked like 100 feet. I didn't just jump feet first like some of the other courageous youth, I dove head first or did a front flip. It wasn't something that everyone did; only a couple of us had the fearlessness to attempt it. So, the question is: were we fearless, brave, courageous and daredevils, or simply AD/H?

When I was only 16 years old, I used to drag race my cars at the Puyallup Raceway and what used to be called Seattle International Raceway (now called Pacific Raceway). My first car was a gorgeous 1967 Camaro Super Sport and my second car was a 1967 Chevelle Super Sport. That was a time when I developed a "need for speed" and enjoyed the adrenaline rush from burning tires and loud exhausts. We also used to race around my hometown of Hoquiam, Washington. The usual spot was the long strip of road to the airport or out on country roads. It seemed like a fun thing to do at the time, but looking back on it, it could have ended badly (not recommended). Being young, I never thought about the risks involved in drag racing and potential damage to my cars, myself or others. That can be one of the downsides to AD/H, we are fearless, but we may not always think things through as methodically as we should. You will notice that "patience" and being "methodical" are not on any list of the attributes of AD/H. Both of those attributes are still "a work in progress" for me, even to this day.

My 1967 Camaro SS   My 1967 Chevelle SS

I had a Yamaha motocross motorcycle in my early 20s, and besides enjoying the thrill of speed, my favorite thing was to jump and see how much hang-time I could get. I would go over any large mound of dirt or gravel I could find that would help catapult me into the air. It was always a calculated risk, but looking back on it, it was mostly a leap of faith each time. Sometimes I landed properly, and other times, not so much. I also used to enjoy standing on the seat and doing wheelies at varying speeds. One day, I was at a gravel pit practicing wheelies and I kept going faster and faster in an effort to keep the front wheel in the air. It was going great until the motorcycle flipped over backwards, and I pounded my body into the gravel at an unreasonably high speed. I was picking gravel out of my back and helmet for a couple of weeks (I was wearing a short sleeve T-shirt – not so bright). I decided it was time to sell the bike before I killed myself (so at least I knew some of my limits).

I started snow skiing at around 13 years old, and I immediately took a liking to jumping and other extreme acts of fearlessness (duh!). When I was in my early 20s I began freestyle skiing, where I competed in mogul skiing, aerials and ballet skiing (looks like ice skating routines, but on short snow skis). I used to do flips off of jumps and helicopters (360's) off of every mogul I could find on the slope.

This is me doing a flip back in 1974. For a height perspective, see the tree top in the lower left corner

One day when I was at Crystal Mountain ski resort, in Washington State, I was taking some jumping lessons from a professional freestyle skier. We built a huge jump right near the chair lift where all the other skiers were in line and waiting for their turn to get to the top of the mountain. My coach chose the location because he thought it would be fun for everyone to watch us perform our feats of glory. He went first and landed a perfect back flip in a full layout position. I had done flips, but all in a tuck position, which makes your body come around faster.

I decided to attempt my first back flip in full layout position. The pro gave me all the instructions and positioned me, so I was about 75 feet up the extremely steep approach ramp from the jump. That would provide me with enough speed to get the air required to complete the rotation of the jump and land safely. Being the fearless AD/H person that I am, I decided that if 75 feet of approach ramp was adequate, then 125 would be even better (OK, it seemed like a good idea at the time). The large crowd started to cheer me on and my adrenaline started to rush as I headed down the steep slope towards the jump.

I hit the lip of the jump, leaned my head back, popped my hips forward exactly the way I had been taught and went sailing through the air at an astounding speed. I must have been 35 feet in the air – it was awesome. But something was wrong – I was in a full layout position and had way more than enough height, but I was not rotating properly. My body had stopped rotating, so my head was facing down and my skis were straight in the air. I floated through the air for what seemed like hours, and then I hit the ground head first. My body collapsed in a heap and my skis came flying off. Out of pure adrenaline rush, I jumped up from the ground, looked back up the hill toward the crowd and saw the look on people's faces. There was the look of terror, and their mouths were moving, but all I could hear was dead silence. I lost my hearing for three days. I woke up on the fourth day, and my hearing was back. The only thing better than being fearless, is to be lucky (and thankful in this case).

I competed in a few slalom water ski events when I was in my 30s, but what I really liked to do was barefoot water ski. This is where you ski, without any skis. You start from a perfectly good slalom ski, pull your rear foot out of the boot and place it in the water, and then kick the ski off your other foot once you are going at least 36 miles-an-hour. If things work as planned, it is an amazing feeling as you skim across the water with a huge rooster tail behind you at the amazement of friends and relatives. However, if it does not work out so well, you will either fall on your ski and cut your face up, or you get lucky, miss the ski and simply hit the water at 36 miles-an-hour with your face (which, by the way, really hurts – it happens so fast you don't even have time to close your eyes). You can also start by floating on your back in the water with nothing more than the skip rope between your legs. The boat takes off at full throttle, and when you get to around 36 miles-an-hour, you stand up on your feet and proudly ski off into the sunset. This is not a sport for the weak at heart and you must be prepared for the agony of defeat. It also leads to badly bruised feet (or face, depending on what took the biggest beating).

Me barefoot water skiing (I still do it)

My other fearless friends and I used to spend all day trying to conjure up risky tricks that we had never done before on the water. We would do five-person pyramids with water skis on (three people on the bottom with skis and two of us would climb up on their shoulders). We tried the six-person pyramid, which is a full pyramid by anyone's standards, but our designated top person chickened out during our attempt, so we abandoned the project. I also tried jumping off of a jet ski going 36 miles an hour with a ski rope in my hand that was connected to a boat also going 36 miles an hour, just to see if I could barefoot from one moving vehicle to another (I highly recommend you do not try this one – we stepped over the line from fearless to stupid on this one). I even jumped off the fly-bridge of a standing 34-foot trawler boat without skis on and barefooted away from it at 36 miles an hour behind a ski boat. By the way, most of my fearless water friendly friends also became entrepreneurs and ended up with successful businesses as well.

Me jumping off the fly bridge and skiing away on my feet
(see the ski rope in my hands)

I skateboarded on occasion up until I was a little over 50 years old, and up until the day I stopped, I used to enjoy riding on my hands. I would find a hill, put both hands on the board, take a few steps and kick up into a handstand and ride the board all the way down the hill. When I play golf, I rarely take the safe shot, I go for the gold and take the shot that no one expects you to make (yes, I lose a lot of balls). Everything I have described in the last couple of paragraphs is just a brief snapshot of the way I live each day – fearless!

I skateboarded on my hands until I was 50 years old.

After I graduated from college in 1975 with a degree in forestry, I came back to my hometown of Hoquiam, Washington and tried to find work in my field. However, it was at a time when the timber industry had just taken a big hit, and times were tough. Since I could not find work in my chosen profession, I found a job in a lumber mill where I worked on what is called the "Green Chain" (pulling wet lumber off of a moving belt and stacking it, in preparation to take it to be kiln dried). One of the foremen who happened to be a great guy, Earl Cummings, asked me what I loved to do in my spare time. I told him I loved snow skiing and water skiing. He said to me *"Why don't you try to make a living out of something you love to do? You are young and even if it doesn't work out, you have lots of time to do something else."*

It was that day, at the age of 20 years old, that I decided to take a risk and open a sporting goods store named "Freestyle Sports," specializing in snow and water skiing. I had absolutely no business experience, nor education on running a business, but I simply did what I always do, I went into fearless mode. I continued to work at the mill in order to earn enough money to start the business. I found a building that was vacant and for lease. I drove to Seattle, met with the owner of the building and signed a three-year lease. Looking back at it, it seemed like an incredibly naive thing to do. Today, there is no way I would sign a three-year lease without a business plan (no plan at all on how I was going to pull this off). As mentioned before, that can be one of the downsides to being "fearless;" sometimes plans don't get enough consideration in the momentum of moving our ideas forward. However, with most people who do not have the gift of fearlessness, they give things too much thought and talk themselves right out of moving forward.

I used each paycheck to buy paint, carpet, fixtures, inventory and anything else I needed to make my dream come true. My dad would come down to my sporting goods store after he worked all day and help me paint, wire lighting and put up fixtures. It took a tremendous amount of creativity to find ways to get a business up and running on a shoestring budget. My dad and I even went out to the bay at Grays Harbor City, found large planks of wood that were now driftwood laying on the shore, and we used a chainsaw to cut each one and make rustic siding for the interior walls of the store. Many of the things that we came up with required tremendous ingenuity in order to pull them off – thank goodness we had two AD/H brains working on the project. It took me about nine months, but the store opened, and my journey as an entrepreneur began. What a fabulous journey it was! I was doing something I loved to do (thank you Earl Cummings!) and learning more about myself in the process. I realized that I loved business, and I loved working with people. Coincidently, Earl's son Rod came to work for me at the store when he was 16 years old, and we have been great friends ever since.

If you look back at just a few of the stories of my life, you can see that fearlessness has always been a part of my life, and I recognized that early on as one of my gifts. As you can read in the last paragraph, my other gifts were starting to slowly appear to me; those of creativity and ingenuity. Since my first entrepreneurial adventure at the age of 20, I have created six other companies from the ground up, which I will talk about in an upcoming chapter.

Once I got away from school and freed myself from the emotional trauma of being labeled with a misguided number that inaccurately measured my talent, I began to see my gifts more clearly. I think it is very hard for many people to see the gifts of AD/H when they are immersed in the struggle for survival of getting through school. It is emotionally painful to try your hardest but be constantly reminded that you are not smart enough (by the education system's standards). Yes, I struggled with that as well, and that is why I am mentioning that I don't think most people with AD/H begin to recognize their gifts until they are adults (and even then, many continue to struggle with the concept that the diagnosis has any gifts to it at all). The further you get away from school and the metrics that labeled you, the easier it gets to rebuild your self-confidence and self-image.

There has been research and plenty of speculation as to how the part of the brain called the Amygdala, might be responsible for why people with AD/H are more fearless. The Amygdala is an almond shaped group of nuclei in the brain, which have long been considered to be directly implicated in processing fear and its emotion memories (storage of memories related to emotional events). The Amygdala communicates with many of the brains' regions, including those that control breathing, heart rate and motor functions. There is some thought that people with AD/H might have a different size Amygdala, resulting in less response to fear and the emotion attached to it. But as with most of the other AD/H research, there are no clear findings that can prove that definitively.

Fearlessness may also be part of our AD/H make-up due to a gene called the DRD4 whose official name is "Dopamine Receptor D4". Dopamine is a neurotransmitter that is produced by the brain. It plays a critical role in the function of the central nervous system and is also linked with the brain's complex system of motivation and reward. Lower levels of this neurotransmitter in the brain may cause a range of symptoms and problems that can be associated with AD/H.

Many of the people with AD/H who are risk-takers may have fewer of the dopamine receptors. This means their brains don't limit the amount of dopamine it produces during activities that would be considered fearless or risky. The result of this is a bigger "high" for these individuals, which motivates them to want to do more of those types of activities, to maintain the high. Risky behavior allows them to artificially produce more dopamine. This may explain why people like me, with AD/H, may be greater risk takers, (which may be why there are so many entrepreneurs who are AD/H). This may also be why we tend to be more susceptible to impulsivity and going into action without thinking things through (there were many times when I should have looked over the landing area before going off a jump on my snow skis – yes, I paid the price).

The fearlessness that I have had all my life has proven to be one of my unique differentiating factors, and that which I believe has made me successful. Even if you look at my primary career today as a professional speaker, it is something that most people cannot do. It is widely written that public speaking is most people's greatest fear. Most people are more afraid of public speaking than they are of being bit by a rattlesnake or dying. Yet, I thrive on being in front of people, and my dream is to one day speak in front of at least 15,000 people. I even get excited just thinking about it, where other people would be projectile vomiting from the thought of it.

Children climbing trees and taking risks scares parents – we only see the bad in it, instead of how that will translate into life skills as they grow older. Do the risks they take make them bad or disruptive children? Or are they the successful entrepreneurs of the future? Are we so busy trying to protect our children from all the ills of the world that we smother them and kill the creativity, ingenuity and fearlessness that is innate within them? Are we stifling their gifts with our own fears and putting limitations on their success?

A gentleman, who was in one of my seminars last year, came up to me after the class and wanted to talk to me. He said his son, who is 21 years old, had been wanting to start up his own business for the last couple of years, but he kept talking his son out of it. It's not that he did not think his son was capable of being successful, but he was trying to protect his son from the potential of failure. He admitted that it was his own fears about failure, and not his son's. He had admittedly been sabotaging his son's attempts to take risks and live his dreams. He said when he got home, he was going to sit his son down and tell him to go after his dreams, and he that he would support his son's decisions.

I have always believed in the saying: The biggest risks bring the biggest rewards. Most people live a mediocre lifestyle, and for some, it is because they enjoy the feelings of security and the safety that it provides. It does not make them wrong; it just makes them different than people like me with the gifts of AD/H. I made the decision that I want to live an extraordinary life, so I have had to be willing to utilize my gift of fearlessness and do things that others would not do. Remember, if you want things that other people do not have, you must be willing to do things that others will not do. Be fearless and go after your dreams regardless of whether you are AD/H or not!

Here are a few of the recognizable celebrities who have, or were thought to have AD/H and the gift of fearlessness:

- Evil & Robbie Knievel
- John F. Kennedy
- Abraham Lincoln
- Christopher Columbus
- Lewis and Clark
- Terry Bradshaw
- Michael Phelps
- Pete Rose
- Nolan Ryan
- Michael Jordan
- Jason Kidd

Chapter 8

The Ultimate Entrepreneurs

If you work at a bank, you are in the financial services industry, but you are in the relationship business.

If you work at a hotel, you are in the hospitality industry, but you are in the relationship business.

If you work at a restaurant, you are in the food services industry, but you are in the relationship business.

If you work at a casino, you are in the entertainment industry, but you are in the relationship business.

If you work at a car dealership, you are in the auto industry, but you are in the relationship business.

People with AD/H tend to be more outgoing and relationship based, which makes them fabulous business people (once again, this will not be true of all people with AD/H). It is especially important if you are an entrepreneur because in most cases, you may be the only salesperson for your company when you are just starting out. The better relationships you build with your community, Chamber of Commerce, bank, vendors, employees and customers, the more successful you will become. Once again, not everyone with AD/H is going to fit the mold of being charismatic and outgoing however; it is very common among people with the diagnosis. That is why people with AD/H are so good at getting people to buy into their vision and be able to move projects forward – sometimes it is simply their passion.

One of the companies I started, Genesis Group, which I will talk about a little further on in this chapter, was a company that performed mystery shopping services. We would send shoppers into different types of businesses to have normal shopping experiences. The shoppers would report the results back to us, and we would present those results to our customers in an effort to evaluate and improve their quality of service.

When the company was just starting out and I had absolutely no customers, I went to a company called "Bon Marche," here in the Seattle area, which is now part of Macy's. I met with the Director of Human Resources, whose name was Ann Nywall. I told her about my great new idea and how it was very unique, and focused on giving positive feedback to employees, not just the negative. I did not hide the fact that I did not have any customers, and that it was a brand new business. I was very passionate about my new idea and rambled on about all my thoughts.

Ann listened to me with intent, and after I was through, she said, *"You have my blessing to offer it to each of the stores."* I went store by store and sold my ideas to each of the 40 managers, and ended up getting all of the stores involved in the program. After about a year of doing business with them, I asked Ann why on earth she ever gave me her blessing since she knew I had never done this type of work before, and she said, *"I knew by your passion that you were going to be good at it."* They were great clients for many years, and she changed the path of my life, for which I will be forever grateful!

My next sales call was to my own bank, which was Seafirst Bank at the time and now it is part of Bank of America. I called my branch and asked who was in charge of quality service for the entire company (about 320 branches at the time). They put me in contact with a fabulous woman, Marie Gunn, at the corporate headquarters in Seattle, who is still a friend to this very day. I met with her and poured out my ideas and concepts for an innovative new mystery shopping program.

When she asked who my clients were, I told her I only had one and it was Bon Marche. It was at that point where she should have probably thrown me out of her office, but she didn't. She put me in touch with the Market Research team, who helped me learn about data processing, and truly guided me through the process of how to operate my company effectively. They were great clients of mine for many years. I asked Marie years later why she hired someone like me who had very little experience, and she said, "*It was your passion and I could see it in your eyes.*"

If I look at all the vendors I have worked with over my 38 years in business, I do business with them because of their personalities, passion and the strong relationships we have built over the years. Even if you are not self-employed, building and sustaining strong relationships is critical to any business. If you are an employee of a company, it is critical that you have strong relationships with the following:

- Your supervisor
- Your peers
- Your customers

If you work for a company and you are in a supervisory role, it is critical that you have good relationships with the following:

- Your supervisor
- Your peers
- Your employees
- Your customers
- Your vendors

If you have the gift of AD/H, then there is a strong possibility you have an innate gift of being able to connect with people and create relationships with those you meet. This is something that pays huge dividends in life and creates a long term annuity for your career and company. Every waking moment of your day should be focused on what you can do to create not only more relationships, but stronger ones as well. If you have the gift – use it!

In the business world, it is very important to have a good balance of talent in your company as you begin hiring people. It is critical to make sure each person's talents are directly related to the skill required for the position. Even though it may feel great to surround yourself with people who agree with everything you say, it is the kiss of death for your company's long-term survival. In most cases, you would not want every employee in your company to have AD/H. Sure, we have many wonderful gifts that will serve your company well, but they're not necessarily great for every position in the company.

Remember, we are fearless and sometimes do not think things through as thoroughly as we should! Would you want your bookkeeper or people in your accounting department to be fearless with your money or not be thorough? Do you want them to do creative accounting and push the limits with your money? Hell no! You want to hire the 4.0 GPA who has a master's degree in accounting and loves dealing with numbers all day long.

Do you want an IT (Information Technology) manager for your company who is fearless and takes risks with your website, servers or internet connections? Do you want to hire a person who does not think things through and just throws new ideas against the wall to see if they stick without talking to you first? I don't think so! There are people in this world who have skills that we do not have, and we need them to be part of our team. This is another case where I would hire the 4.0 GPA with a degree in network administration and minor in programming instead of the fun loving person with AD/H.

When it comes to hiring people for sales, marketing and advertising, people with the gifts of AD/H shine brightly. This is their wheelhouse and where they will also be the happiest. These are jobs that fit my hiring philosophy, "Hire the smile and train the skill" very well. You want people who are charismatic, outgoing, passionate, relationship builders who are fearless in their pursuits, creative in their methods and ingenious in their approach. Once again, here are the gifts.

- Fearlessness
- Creativity

- Ingenuity

As mentioned, there are certain jobs that are best suited for people with AD/H. Most of those require creativity and ingenuity, along with the freedom to be active (especially if you are the hyper type). Most people with the diagnosis of AD/H like fast-paced work environments, so they do not get bored or lose interest. Here are just a few jobs that may be well suited for people who have AD/H:

- Airline Industry (Flight attendant, ticket counter, baggage handler but definitely NOT pilots)
- Auto Mechanic
- Bartender
- Chef
- Construction
- Delivery Business (UPS Driver, USPS, Messenger Services)
- Emergency Medical Technicians
- Entertainment
  - Actor
  - Comedian (especially improv)
  - Dancer
  - Film Maker
  - Game Show Host
  - Producer
  - Writer
- Graphic Artist
- Interior Design
- Law Enforcement
- Marketing
- Motivational Speaker
- Pastor
- Photographer

- Politician
- Public Relations
- Publishing
- Radio (great DJs)
- Real Estate Agent
- Retail
- Sales of any sort
- Server (food and beverage)
- Teacher (PE if you are hyper)
- Television
- Trainer
- Wall Street Trader
- Web Design

One of the gifts we offer to the world is our innate ability to build companies and employ people. We 2.47 GPA people build businesses and then hire other 2.47 people, along with 4.0 people to work for us in positions that require their skill set. We do not discriminate against grade point average because we know that it takes many different talents to execute the vision.

The differences between people who are 4.0 GPA and 2.47 GPA are not about:

- Good vs. Bad
- True vs. False
- Angelic vs. Evil
- Right vs. Wrong
- Correct vs. Incorrect
- Superior vs. Inferior

No one has to be made wrong. It is recognizing the differences and embracing each of our own gifts. We are all needed on this earth, and we all serve an important role. My obvious frustration with the traditional public education system is its lack of recognition for people like myself, who are very smart, but simply don't have the skill to retain and recall information upon command (which is most of what school is about). Why can't we find a way to grade all of us on our own unique gifts and not just the gifts that the education system has declared are important (such as a good memory)?

I believe many of us with AD/H are born business savvy, but sometimes, we just don't discover it until later in life when we are full-fledged adults. Once the cloud of uncertainty about our gifts wears off, we can move our lives forward in the direction we were destined to go. The great thing about being an entrepreneur is that once you build a company doing something you love, you will never have to work another day in your life. Because when you are doing what you love to do, it does not feel like work. It feels like you are getting paid to do what you are passionate about.

The toughest part about being self-employed for some of us is having the self-discipline to take time off and not work. It is so easy to get wrapped up in the fun of work that you forget to have a well-balanced life, which consists of spending time with your family and friends. It is very easy to become a workaholic because it does not feel like work to you. However, everyone else in your life may notice your absence, so pay close attention to the emotional needs of others as well. Even though it is gratifying to be considered a great entrepreneur, it pales in comparison to being considered a great friend, father, mother, husband, wife or significant other.

Here is the abbreviated journal of my journey as an entrepreneur. Which began with "Freestyle Sports," the first business I started in 1975 when I was 20 years old.

Even without much knowledge of the business world I ran my ski shop successfully for three years, and when the lease came due in 1978, the landlord would not renew my lease. I had done such a great job of fixing up the building that they wanted to use the space for their own real estate business. I was forced into the choice of either relocating and building my ski shop up from scratch again, or maybe trying to find a way to learn more about the business world and seeking further education.

One of many serendipitous moments in my life occurred about that time when I picked up our local newspaper and it had a "Help Wanted Ad" looking for a store manager for a new store in Aberdeen. It was for a company called Squire Shop, which was a clothing store chain with more than 20 locations throughout Washington and Oregon. I contacted them, they interviewed me, and I got the phone call a week later that they wanted me to start work on Monday (the call came on a Thursday).

However, they said they wanted me to manage the Everett Mall store, which was a 2.5 hour drive from where I lived, not the Aberdeen store. I still had my ski shop to liquidate, so I had no idea how I was going to manage both jobs at the same time, but I said yes (once again, something that AD/H people are very good at – moving fearlessly forward without sometimes having all the answers).

I worked at the Squire Shop six days a week, and 12 hours a day, while at the same time, my fabulous mother and some of my friends helped to liquidate my ski shop for me in their spare time. On my only day off, I would drive back to the ski shop and work 18 or more hours mounting bindings and doing all the shop work that needed to be done then drive back to Everett that night to get a few hours of sleep before work. Needless to say, it was exhausting, but after about six weeks, we finally got the ski shop inventory sold, and I was free to begin my new journey.

I worked for the Squire Shop for a little over three years and managed five different stores. I learned so much about how companies were run, and I had many ideas about how they could even be run better. I used to go to the corporate office and work with the accounting department to help design better daily accounting standards for the stores. I loved the operations side and enjoyed finding a better mousetrap for anything that was not working perfectly. When the company had a store in trouble, they sent me in to retrain everyone and get it back on track.

When a new mall was being built, and they had a new store to open, they sent me because I was very organized and resourceful. A few of my AD/H gifts were unfolding at the age of 24 years old. I was already aware of my fearlessness, but the curiosity muscle that comes along with creativity and ingenuity was being flexed, and I loved it. I actually felt smart for the first time and was starting to get convinced that maybe my grades in school were wrong. Maybe I was actually smarter than the education system gave me credit for – my confidence started to grow.

As my confidence grew in business and my self-image started to improve, I also noticed that I was becoming more confident with women. I never had a girlfriend in high school and did not date much because I was terrified I would get turned down if I asked someone out. My self-image and self-worth were very low, and most of it came from not feeling "good enough" based on my low grades and struggles in school. So, I figured that if I tried hard to get a girlfriend, I would probably do poorly at that as well (poor rationale, but it seemed reasonable at the time). With my new-found belief and confidence in "me," I began to enjoy a very robust social life, along with my career. As I have said throughout this book, the one gift every child and adult should be given is that of confidence – it changes careers and lives.

In 1981, a smaller competitor of Squire Shop contacted me, and I interviewed with the owner. The company was Jeans Warehouse and they had four stores in the local Seattle area. They hired me as the operations manager, which was right up my alley because I loved the diversity of the job and the fast paced nature of the work (which is true of many people with AD/H). The company was an absolute mess; with no systems or procedures for handling money, inventory or people – it was a dream job for me because I could actually make a difference.

It was a lot of fun, but a lot of work, and there was so much I could do to help this company be better. I ended up also taking over the responsibility of overseeing the merchandise buyers. I got to travel to New York and Los Angeles for the first time in my life and work with vendors. I was getting exposed to new parts of the business world that I had not previously experienced. I was more involved in the finances of the company, advertising and Human Resources; my hands touched just about every part of the company.

When the President of Jeans Warehouse left in 1983, I was promoted, and became the President of the company at 29 years of age. One of the gifts I have already mentioned in the book is the ability for many people with AD/H to be charismatic and possess good people skills. We naturally gravitate towards the top and end up in leadership roles because of our unique talent for emotional intelligence, which is the ability to identify, assess, and control the emotions of oneself, of others, and of groups. Do not minimize this gift in yourself if you have it, because it is a unique differentiating factor that will separate you from the crowd and provide you with amazing opportunities. I grew the company from four to seven stores and had it very profitable during my tenure.

In 1984, I was approached by one of our clothing vendors, a gentleman named David McRoberts, and he asked if I wanted to work for a company in which he was a partner. The company was called McKenzie Bend, and it was based in Eugene, Oregon where they manufactured women's sportswear. They were looking for someone to be their merchandise manager and oversee the designers. It was something I had no experience in, but once again, being AD/H, I took the leap of faith in myself and moved fearlessly into a new career on the wholesale side of the garment business. I never focused on what I "did not know," I simply used what I "did know" as a compass to guide me. This was foreign territory to me because everything was new, but I loved the adventure.

I flew to New York and Los Angeles, looked at what was happening on the streets and in the stores in terms of fashion trends. I went shopping for what are called "piece goods" in order to find great fabrics from which we could make innovative clothing (remember, I am AD/H and have the gift of creativity and ingenuity, so this was fun). I had fabric samples mailed back to the designers in Eugene with my ideas as to what to possibly do with those fabrics. In those days, we would make clothes out of perfectly fine fabrics and then send them off to Los Angeles to have them stone-washed or over-dyed, so they looked worn out and old.

I wanted to increase our average sale and give women a reason to buy more of our products. So I suggested we use some of the fabric scraps that might normally get thrown out when making shirts and pants and make matching accessories. We created handbags, vests and other accessories, and we coordinated everything so buyers would have no choice but to buy additional items (because they all went together). We also gave some of the smaller items away for free as incentive for the buyers to purchase more. In other words, if they bought the pants with the matching vest, you would get the matching hand-bag for free. The company doubled their sales during my first season.

The company was bought by another company, based in San Francisco. They asked me to move down with the company and continue my work with them. I was just getting ready to start a family, and when I looked at the high cost of living in San Francisco, compared to the lower cost of living in Seattle, I turned the offer down. However, David McRoberts, who had just sold his share of the McKenzie Bend company, asked me if I was interested in starting up a company with him. The idea of being self-employed again was very intriguing to me because I now had business knowledge and expertise that I did not have when I opened my sporting goods store. After my many recent successes, I was beaming with confidence and feeling pretty good about me (which was a pretty big change for the guy who never felt "good enough").

David and I got together and discussed what type of company we could start. We wanted a product that targeted women, since they are more voracious consumers than men. We wanted it to be something they would buy a lot of, and find it almost a necessity purchase. We wanted it to be something that women bought frequently and could provide us with good profit margins. We decided that pantyhose fit our plan perfectly, so in 1985, we started Volt Hosiery. David had connections with a company out of Montreal, Canada, which had packaging that was very unique. There was a swatch of the fabric on the outside of the package which would allow women to touch and feel the hosiery without having to tear it open. It was innovative, which was exactly what we wanted.

It was an industry that neither of us had any experience in, but once again, fearlessness, creativity and ingenuity led the way. Looking back on it, I think David was AD/H too because he was also a serial entrepreneur who was extremely creative and fearless. Together, we were a pretty good team when it came to innovation. We wanted the pantyhose to have a name that sounded sophisticated, like… "Rothschild"… "Vanderbilt"… or "Kennedy." We ended up taking David's name and my name and combining them into:

VOLT HOSIERY
A "David Bradley Designer Collection"

My legal name is actually Brad, not Bradley, but we tweaked my name to give it a more sophisticated feel. I still chuckle when I see that name because neither of us knew crap about pantyhose when we started. But we did know business, and we knew what people wanted. The packaging was a hit and combined with some very innovative displays that we designed and had manufactured locally, we were now in the hosiery business nationwide.

Volt Hosiery with the innovative packaging and displays

With every company I was involved in, I learned a valuable lesson, which helped me craft future ventures. What I learned from the hosiery business was that it was very inventory intensive and required the banks to finance our growth. We had 27 colors, 25 unique styles and four different sizes in each, so controlling inventory was a nightmare. David handled, the financing and I ran the day to day operations, which included sales management. This required a lot of travel because I had to hire sales reps for all 50 states and travel to all the major markets for the trade shows that were endless.

The travel took me away from home quite a bit, and since our son was just about a year old, being gone was very hard on me and the entire family. I came home one time from a trip and jumped in to help my wife with our son and some of the chores, and I will never forget when she said *"It is really hard when you come home and mess up our schedule."* Shortly thereafter (in 1990), I sold my share of the business to my partner David and moved on to my next adventure. I realized that part of my new business plan had to include better work-life balance; otherwise, success just wasn't worth it.

While I was near the end of the hosiery business, my wife and I started a children's shirt company called "PooWear" (named after our cat "Poo"), that specialized in cute animal characters, combined with funny sayings. I was always coming up with funny or sarcastic things that children might say (once again, utilizing the creative AD/H in me), and my wife was a good artist, so we combined our talents to create this new company. However, the real creativity was the ink we used in the printing process. It was a new type of ink at the time called "Puff Ink," which when heated (immediately after printing), raised or "puffed up" to give the shirt a three dimensional look and texture that had never been seen before in printed shirts.

We came up with innovative designs and packaging, so we could separate ourselves from our competition. I even approached an author, Stephen Cosgrove, who had a very successful children's book series called "Serendipity," to license that name for our products. Once again, I had absolutely no prior experience in the children's shirt market or with how to license products, but thank goodness for AD/H, that did not prevent me from moving fearlessly forward. After only one year, someone made us an offer to buy our company. It was not our plan to sell it that fast, however, it was clear to me that it was also turning into an inventory nightmare and had some of the same trappings as the pantyhose business.

PooWear children's shirt company with "Puff-Ink"

The next company was a brainchild of mine, which was created to help businesses increase employee productivity and profitability, which I named Genesis Group. The word "Genesis" means "new beginning" and I wanted to create a company that was an accumulation of my years of business experience and wisdom. Here were the business lessons I had learned so far from my previous business adventures:

- **No seasonal businesses** (lesson from Freestyle Sports)
- **No inventory** (lesson from Jeans Warehouse, Volt Hosiery & PooWear)
- **No bank financing** (lesson from Volt Hosiery & PooWear)
- **No employees** (lesson from all my companies)
- **No business partner** (lesson from Volt Hosiery)

- **No high operating overhead** (lesson from all my companies)

When I created Genesis Group back in 1990 at the age of 36, my vision was to have a company that evaluated the level of service my clients were offering their customers. I would measure the service by sending friends and relatives, whom I thought had a good appreciation for what good customer service is, into my client's locations and have them perform mystery shops. They would act like regular customers, but employees would not know the shoppers would be reporting on their performance. Then, my shoppers would complete a questionnaire that asked them to score the level of service they received, and I would present that to my clients in a monthly report. The client would present the results to their employees and coach them on how to improve their performance. This was truly an idea that I conjured up after being in retail for many years, but I did not know that mystery shopping had been used for many years prior to me (however, up until that time, mostly for security purposes). When I started Genesis Group, if you typed "mystery shopping" into a search engine, only myself and three other companies appeared (four total hits). Today if you type in those same words, you will get more than 23,700 hits.

Genesis Group was created from my imagination in 1990 and sold in 2002

I went through my above list of things that I did not want in my new business. Genesis Group fit the mold because it was a service oriented business by design. It was perfect because it was not seasonal, I would not need any inventory, I would not need any bank financing, I would not need any employees (this turned out to be wrong – oops!), I would not need a business partner, and I could work from home and keep my overhead low (this also turned out to be wrong – oops again!).

Besides being a mystery shopping company that evaluated service, I was asked back in 1991 to consult on how to improve service and train employees on how to perform better. Even though I was terrified of public speaking most of my life, it was really easy and fun to do when I was speaking about something I was passionate about. Customer service and leadership development were two things I was very passionate about, which eventually turned me into one of the top trainers in the world.

In order to grow my business rapidly and not need bank financing, I needed to apply my AD/H gifts of creativity and ingenuity and come up with an innovative idea. One of the business philosophies that I learned along my journey in the world of sales was, you will never know unless you ask. Based on that philosophy, I decided to be fearless and try something that I did not know was acceptable or even possible.

When clients asked what my payment terms were, I told them they would need to pay me in advance, at the beginning of each month, which they did without hesitation. The first time I told a client my terms, I waited for them to pounce on me with the words *"Are you nuts!"* but it never happened – ever! I had a very large national bank client at the time that used to pay me three months at a time, in advance. They would send me a check for $250,000 and I would deposit it into a money market account, draw interest and pull funds whenever I needed it. It is interesting how I swore I would never have a company that needed bank financing – as it turned out, that bank client did finance me, but I got the interest income and not them ☺. That was a great lesson in my life, which I hope you will remember as well, it's simple: "you will never know until you ask."

The company was extremely successful, creating the need for 35 full-time employees, employee benefits, 3,500 square feet of expensive office space, office equipment, $300,000 in copy machines, 35 computers, servers, programmers and the list goes on and on. Even though it was very successful, it was incredibly stressful. I found most of my days involved managing my company and dealing with employee issues, more than doing what I loved to do, which was being a professional speaker. I wanted to get back to my original focus of not having employees or high overhead. I wanted to have a company that was solely reliant on my talents and not those of others. I decided to sell Genesis Group to a company out of Houston Texas in 2002.

Even though I had sold my company, and I was no longer in the mystery shopping industry, I was elected as the President of the Mystery Shopping Providers Association for 2002 (www.mysteryshop.org). I helped take annual revenues from about $44,000 to over $250,000 with some creative new ideas for the industry, which were implemented by other very successful MSPA members (who were also AD/H). I was also inducted into the mystery shopping "Hall of Fame," which is the highest honor in the industry. As I have said before, many of us with the gift of AD/H rise to the top of organizations and are looked to for our leadership, fearlessness, creativity and ingenuity.

My next company was simply a hybrid of Genesis Group; I named it Brad Worthley International. It would continue to perform consulting and training services, just like Genesis Group however, we would not offer mystery shopping services. I was also going to get my final two priorities right this time by not having any employees and also working from home and keeping my overhead low. Finally, in 2002, with the seamless introduction of Brad Worthley International into the market, I got all of my objectives fulfilled.

- **No seasonal businesses**
- **No inventory**
- **No bank financing**
- **No employees**

- **No business partner**
- **No high operating overhead**

Nailed it!

Our mission today at Brad Worthley International is: helping organizations create service cultures, a place where employees love to work and customers love to do business. Our primary business is leadership development and customer service training. But, we also offer complimentary services like pre-employment evaluations for sales, service and leadership. We offer leadership developmental assessments to help quantify a person's leadership strengths and weaknesses. We also provide employee surveys and customer surveys, so you can inspect what you expect. You can learn more about my company by visiting www. BradWorthley.com

BRAD WORTHLEY
INTERNATIONAL

In order to fulfill my vision of not having employees, I had to be very realistic and resourceful as to what tasks I would do and what tasks I would sub-contract out to other people. I wanted to stay focused on my AD/H gifts and have other people perform the tasks that they are good at (their gifts). I have external vendors who do my website development, graphic art work, accounting, book editing, printing and data entry. I have been doing this for more than 11 years, and it has worked perfectly!

At the same time I was running Brad Worthley International, I also worked to create a new company called "A Prophecy." The intent was to create an innovative on-line pre-employment testing system that would make the hiring process easier and more accurate for my clients. After six months of development, I abandoned this on-line system in favor of a new relationship with a testing firm with far more expertise than I had. The new firm that I developed a great relationship with had more than 30 years of expertise with proven products that eliminated all of the studies and testing that would have been required with my own system. Instead of trying to reinvent the wheel (which those of us with AD/H are very good at), it was very clear that they had the perfect product already, so that is why I utilize their services today. The pre-employment evaluations are available on my website at: www.BradWorthley.com/services/pre-employment-evaluations.

The last of my creative adventures to date is an on-line system that helps facilitate the coaching process, and it is called "The Focus Coaching System" (www.FocusCoachingSystem.com). The Focus Coaching System is an online paperless coaching system used to simplify the coaching process. The Focus Coaching System does not replace traditional in-person or telephone coaching, it facilitates it. People who are life coaches, personal coaches, AD/H Coaches, leadership coaches or executive coaches can utilize this system to facilitate and enhance the coaching experience. This powerful online system gives people the freedom to coach from anywhere in the world without lugging files around. Whether they are coaching one person or hundreds, The Focus Coaching System will save coaches a tremendous amount of time and make the entire coaching process easier for them <u>and</u> their clients. This business is still alive and well.

As you can see, my entrepreneurial adventures have spanned 39 years as of the writing of this book and taken many paths. Why is it that I was able to create businesses in my head and turn them into reality, where others would never be willing to take the risk? Think how many people have great ideas but will never turn them into a reality because they lack the fearlessness to push them forward. I truly believe that none of these businesses would have been created if it were not for the gifts of creativity, ingenuity and fearlessness – which are just some of the gifts of AD/H that I am grateful for.

Chapter 9

People Don't Fail, Systems Do

I do not believe that people fail as much as systems do, so it is important for anyone with AD/H to have great systems in place to help reduce failure. Systems do not have to be complex software or hardware; they can be simple in nature, yet effective.

In all of my businesses, whenever we had failure of any sort, I rarely asked "*Who did it?*" because that was not truly important to me. What I really cared about is, "*What systems are we going to put into place to make sure this never happens to any of us again?*" Our role as leaders should be to keep our employees physically and emotionally safe. Employees do not come to work wanting to fail, which is emotionally traumatizing, so we must do everything we can to help them be successful and build their confidence.

The same theory goes for our children. No child goes to school wanting to fail. As adults, our role as parents, teachers and administrators should be to keep children physically and emotionally safe. With as much trauma as we have in our schools today trying to keep children physically safe (with illness, bullies, predators and weapons as only a few of examples), keeping them emotionally safe is far harder.

What are we going to do as a nation to create good systems in our schools that will allow our children to feel emotionally safe, confident and encouraged to want to learn? What systems can we put into place that will not only help educate our students, but help build their self-confidence as well? I not only think it is important, I might even suggest that it could be even more important than the curriculum itself in being successful in their careers and life.

As parents, what systems are we willing to put into place in our homes to help keep our children physically and emotionally safe? How active are we willing to become in our children's education in order to help them be successful? The traditional public education system, as broken as I believe it is, is there to educate your children, but not be a parent to your children. I can only imagine that teachers must get incredibly frustrated with the lack of parental involvement or the indifference some parents have about their own child's education. These children need our time and attention if they are going to be successful. Don't ever assume that the education system is taking care of all of their intellectual, spiritual, physical and emotional needs. That is not all their job, it is our job as parents, so "active parenting" is also a requirement for healthy and confident children.

My wife and I were very active in our son's school and sporting activities. I was his soccer and baseball coach when he was 5 years old until he was about 14 years old. I went to every parent teacher meeting and school event, except for the rare day I was out of town on business. My wife and I would read to and with my son every night when he was in grade school. We helped him with his homework when needed, and we were very present during his school years.

With that said, we noticed when he was in about fifth grade, when we asked him to read to us, he was slow and awkward. He seemed to struggle with his words and would fidget as he was reading, like he wanted to escape this painful task. We decided to take him to a Sylvan Learning Center and have him tested to see what they thought of his reading skills. The results showed that our son was two years behind in reading, and I was shocked.

I went to his school the very next day and showed his teacher the results, and she said *"Yes, that's about right."* I asked her why in all of the parent teacher meetings we had had over the last year that she did not tell me about his challenges. She said that since the school district did not have special programs to help our son, she did not see a need to mention it since there was nothing they could do. I then went into the Principal's office and confronted her about it as well, and she said the same thing – nothing we can do, so why tell you. REALLY?

We realized that if he could not read proficiently, it would not only impact his reading grades, but math, science and every other class he had as well. This is one of the first signs we had that he might have AD/H. We enrolled him in Sylvan for one year, and he got his reading skills up to a grade level above his own. It built his confidence back up, and we put better systems in place at home to make sure this would never happen to us again. We monitored his homework closer, kept in better contact with the teachers and demanded answers when needed. We also had more conversations with our son as to how he felt about his progress in certain subjects. It was finally in seventh grade that we had him tested for AD/H because we were alert, paying attention and involved in our son's education.

Children with AD/H need strong systems in place to help them be successful and to keep their self-confidence up. The same is true of adults, but once you become an adult, you are far more aware of your strengths and weaknesses and able to deal with them on your own. I believe it is one of the reasons that, as an adult, I have not felt a lot of pain from AD/H, because I have spent years creating good systems to help me be successful. As parents, we need to do our due diligence and help our children put good systems in place as well.

Results of good systems:

- Less stress
- Less failure
- Less frustration
- Greater success

- Greater confidence
- Greater productivity

Routine and structure are very important non-pharmaceutical solutions in the world of AD/H, because most of us function better when we have a consistent routine or structure that we follow (routines and structure are simply good systems). This helps reduce the possibility of failure and requires far less mental energy. The goal is to work diligently to create positive behavior habits, because habits require no mental energy (require no thought because they are automated). However, it does require a certain amount of discipline (which does require thought and energy) to create positive habits.

One of the most important habits you can develop is being a list maker. It will keep you from forgetting what you need to do, plus you can prioritize your tasks, which is also very important. I would suggest that you always keep paper and pen handy; any thought that pops into your head, write it down before you forget it. I have a notepad next to my laptop on my office desk, so I can move any task or thought to paper, which keeps me organized and helps reduce my stress. If I remember that I need to get a gallon of milk at the store, I write it down immediately. If I thought about a new idea for a book or seminar, I write it down at that moment. If a client calls and asks me to send them a report, I write it down, but I also always ask, *"When do you need it?"* so I can prioritize it accordingly.

I also have a notepad in my nightstand in our bedroom, so if my brain starts getting creative in the middle of the night, I can drain my brain and get back to sleep. If I do not write it down, then I lose sleep by lying awake and trying to remember whatever it is. I also have paper and pen in my car, because my narrator loves a good car ride and has many opinions about the world it sees from the highways and byways. It wants to be heard, and it does not want me discounting or forgetting its words of wisdom. If I do not write the narrator's pearls down, I will more than likely forget them by the time I get to where I am driving.

When I get home, I move my notes from the car over to my main task sheet next to my laptop, so I only have one list to prioritize. I put both personal and professional items on my list (instead of having multiple lists). At the end of each day before I leave my office, I drain my brain of anything else that I can think of that needs consideration the next day. Then, I prioritize my task list for the next day. I do this, so I do not wake up at 5 in the morning and start thinking about what I need to do when I get into the office, which ruins my sleep. Instead, I drain my brain and prioritize my list the night before, so I do not have to think about it until I get to my office in the morning. When I arrive, I just look at my list, select item number one, and start working.

One of the steps to my prioritizing process is always picking the most important thing that needs to be done first thing in the morning – not the most fun thing to do. I consider what will provide me with the greatest return on my investment of time, whether it is greater customer advocacy, employee advocacy, sales, productivity or profitability. If you are AD/H, then you are probably prone to wanting to do tasks that you are good at because it makes you feel good about you (which we need from time to time). You are also very good at procrastination and getting distracted by doing other things that bring you joy. That is why it is critical that you not only create "to do" lists, but prioritize them properly as well in order to stay focused.

I would suggest that you only prioritize as many tasks as you believe you can accomplish the next day. Never prioritize more than you truly believe you can do. Let's say you prioritized 10 things on your list, but only got half of them done – how do you feel about your success for the day? Do you feel accomplished? Do you feel like you were productive and got a lot done? Probably not! Even though it may sound like a game you are playing with yourself, it is important to do everything in your power to feel accomplishment, feel good about you and help build your confidence. If you set two goals and get both of them done by 3 o'clock, then it will feel good to you. Celebrate, and then maybe get one more task done as well, which means you did more than you set out to do. This is not only a good exercise if you are AD/H, but this is a great exercise for anyone.

In the process of creating tasks or setting goals for ourselves, we sometimes set ourselves up for failure by setting goals that are not S.M.A.R.T. Whether they are personal or professional goals; make sure they are well thought out:

- **S**pecific
- **M**easurable
- **A**chievable
- **R**ealistic
- **T**imed

As an example, if I told you that I wanted to reduce my stress, would that be a S.M.A.R.T. goal? Of course not, and one of the reasons is because it is not specific enough. Stress is a big subject and can have many causes, so by simply saying you want to set a goal to reduce your stress; you might be setting yourself up for failure. It may also be hard to measure and difficult to achieve without being more specific, which can also make it unrealistic. There was also no timeframe attached to the goal. The real key to setting S.M.A.R.T. goals is what specifically are you going to do to make your goals become a reality, and when will they be achieved?

Let's try this again and make stress reduction a S.M.A.R.T. goal this time: I have now taken the time to determine that my stress is simply a "symptom" and the "problem" that is causing my stress, is my desk is a mess. The desk in my office is messy, which has me feeling disorganized and is therefore stressing me out. Let's say today is Monday, and my goal is to reduce my stress by cleaning and organizing my desk by 5 p.m. this Friday. Is that now a S.M.A.R.T. goal? Let's analyze it and see:

- **S**pecific – *Yes, because it is isolated specifically to my desk.*
- **M**easurable – *Yes, because once I am done, I can see my desk is clean and organized.*
- **A**chievable – *Yes, because it is something that I can easily accomplish in the time allowed.*

- **R**ealistic – *Yes, because it is a real and practical goal.*
- **T**imed – *Yes, because I set a very specific time-line to complete it by 5 p.m. Friday.*

Even though many of you might be good goal setters, which one of the above five criteria do you think most people fail to attach to their goals? If you guessed "Timed," you are right. Why do you think many people do not set a time frame for completing their goals? It is because they have a fear of failure, so they are trying to protect themselves from the emotional pain of failure. If you don't set a specific time and date for your goals, then you can't feel like a failure if you don't get it done on time.

The problem is; you are not holding yourself accountable, and in the process, you set yourself up for failure because you may not attain your goals. Letting yourself off the hook is not a good thing. You must hold yourself to the highest standards if you want to achieve your goals. With that said, you certainly should make sure that the time frame you set for yourself is realistic and achievable. ALWAYS set a very specific date and time for your goals, and you will find that you will achieve them. Why? Because most people fear failure so much that if they set a specific date and time, they will achieve it because they do not want to fail.

Setting S.M.A.R.T. goals is a great system to make you more pro-ductive and focused, which will actually reduce the chances of failure. Creating a specific time-frame creates commitment, accountability and also reduces procrastination. This builds confidence and the cycle of success begins!

Here are examples of just a few systems to help you manage your AD/H:

❖ **Reduce distractions.**

  ▪ If you are working on a task, either at work or at home, you might consider removing potential distractions from your environment. If you have a window in your office, it will probably pull your attention away and distract you each time someone walks by, so close the blinds or curtains. Close your office door, so people walking by or coworkers talking in the office don't distract you. You might consider pushing the "DND" (Do Not Disturb) button on your phone for a few hours, so the telephone does not divert you away from work. Maybe consider earplugs during times when you need intense concentration. If something pulls your attention away from your work, don't ignore it; find a solution to reduce the distraction immediately (remember, you like to procrastinate).

❖ **Record your thoughts.**

- It is critical to get important ideas or tasks out of your head and written down. However, you may not always have paper and pen handy, which can lead to a systems failure. Most of us have our mobile phone with us throughout the day, so you can always use your phone to either make a quick note (if you have the proper app), text yourself a quick message or simply call and leave yourself a voice mail. If it is work related, you can call your work number and leave the message there, so when you get back to your office, your thoughts or tasks are waiting for you. You can also buy an inexpensive digital recorder that is the size of a pen and record your thoughts at any time. This is great if you fly or are in the car a lot. You can ramble on into your digital recorder and listen later at your convenience.

❖ **Create rituals that soothe you.**

- Rituals can be good for those of us with AD/H, so sometimes creating a good working or learning environment can help us be more productive. Lighting candles in your office, having water features that provide gentle background noise, soft music, aroma therapy that provides stimulation, photo collages of family and friends or anything else that creates a space that allows you to relax and stay focused should be considered.

❖ **Behavior systems to remind us.**

- You might consider creating behavior systems that help stimulate thought or remind you of things that need to be done. As an example, when I light a candle on my credenza (which is away from my desk, so I cannot see it), I take the lid off the candle jar and set it next to my car keys/wallet/mobile phone on my desk. This will remind me to blow the candle out before I leave my desk at the end of the day.

- When I need to remember something short term (like in the next 10 to 15 minutes), I extend one finger if I am trying to remember one thought, or two fingers if I am trying to remember two things. I sometimes do this when I am in our spa relaxing, but my narrator is still in creativity mode. If I get an idea or thought and have no paper or pen handy to write it down, I will simply extend a finger or two until I get back inside the house and am able to write it down.

- If you are trying to remember to take your medication, set it near your toothbrush, shaver, bathroom sink, car keys or someplace where you are guaranteed to see it. Also, set your mobile phone or watch alarm to go off at the time you want to take your meds.

❖ **Set S.M.A.R.T. goals for yourself.**

- As described earlier, it helps you think through your goals more clearly in order to increase your chances of success.

❖ **Use sticky notes for quick reminders.**

- Use sticky notes to remind you of impending appointments or tasks (within 24 hours). However, use them sparingly because too many sticky notes become ineffective reminders. Also, having the same sticky note on your desk for long periods is ineffective; it will eventually become invisible to you. That is why I suggest using them for 24-hour tasks or reminders.

❖ **Use a highlight pen when reading books.**

- If you are AD/H, you already know that reading is not one of your favorite past-times, in most cases. Highlight words, sentences or paragraphs that are meaningful to you as you read. This will allow you to go back through and re-read the highlighted parts of the book again (to assist in retention), which takes far less time. This is not a good idea with library or borrowed books ☺.

❖ **Systems of rewards for completing goals.**

- If you set a S.M.A.R.T. goal for yourself and you achieve it, set a small reward for yourself. It can be something as simple as a bubble bath, bottle of your favorite wine, dinner at your favorite restaurant or a massage. Celebrate the small victories!

❖ **Writing thoughts down so you don't forget.**

- As mentioned previously, one of the most powerful tools for someone with AD/H is a pen and paper. Reduce your stress and increase your productivity by writing your thoughts down. If you are more high tech, you can use your mobile phone and an app that allows note taking.

❖ **Good filing system to increase organization.**

- Create well organized filing systems using a file cabinet, hanging folders, file folders that are clearly labeled with a labeling machine. You can also use plastic bins that are labeled and easy to find. Organize your files by what makes sense to you, not necessarily by what might make sense to others. If you have a file folder with directions and warranty information from a new spa that you just purchased, you might label it by the company name or the word "spa" or "hot tub." Pick a word to file it under that is your natural "go-to" word. Organization helps prevent failure and also reduces stress.

❖ **Plan meals in order to save money and eat healthier.**

- People with AD/H tend to be more "on the fly" or impulsive and less planned. You can eat healthier and save a ton of money by planning your meals on a weekly basis. That way you tend to buy only groceries you need to make complete well balanced meals. This approach is far better and cheaper than having a lot of groceries in the pantry that don't create meals.

❖ **Have good systems in place to be an "Active Listener".**

- Being attentive is not one of your gifts. Be an active listener by leaning forward in your chair, elbows on the table, pen and paper in hand (or use a laptop) and be a good note taker. Remember attention deficit means you have a difficult time paying attention, so "active" listening helps keep you engaged in meetings.

❖ **Open your mail each day and be decisive about it as you open it.**

- AD/H can lead to procrastination in some people, which can lead to junk piles and stress. Do not let piles build up – open your mail and be decisive about what you are doing with each one. Decide if it is garbage, gets filed, gets put in the payables file or gets added to your priority list.

❖ **Set your car keys on top of your wallet/purse and cell phone.**

- There are two things that you will not want to forget when you leave your house in a hurry, and they are your wallet/ purse and your cell phone. If you lay your keys on top of those two items in your house (on a desk or counter in a consistent location), the chances of you forgetting them will go down dramatically.

❖ **Keep an accurate check book register and balance it monthly.**

- People with AD/H tend to not pay attention to the details, so make sure that you keep an accurate checkbook and balance it monthly with your bank statements. This will help you avoid bank overdraft fees, bounced checks, late payments, bad credit scores and embarrassing moments. If finances are not your strong suit, then purchase a software program like Intuit's "QuickBooks" to organize your finances and help you balance your checking account each month.

❖ **Keeping things you use frequently in the same place all the time.**

- Routine and consistency are very important, so everything should have a place and be in that place. Place things in the first place that pops into your mind, so when you are looking for it in the future, the first place that pops into your head will be the place where it is (even if it does not make sense to other people).

❖ **Make "to do" lists and prioritize your list at the end of every day.**

- Making lists helps reduce the possibility of forgetting, plus it provides a good tool to help you prioritize your tasks each day. This was discussed in detail earlier in this chapter, so you may even want to re-read it – very important!

❖ **Break large tasks up into smaller ones, so it does not seem so overwhelming.**

- You may become overwhelmed with a large project, which might thrust you right into procrastination mode (analysis causes paralysis). If a project feels insurmountable or gives you anxiety because you are not sure where to start, take a deep breath, and then break it down into bite size pieces and steps that make sense to you. Then focus on one step at a time until it is complete.

❖ **Be decisive – do not let tasks build up – make decisions and deal with them now.**

  ▪ You may be prone to putting things off because you simply don't want to make a decision on it. Remember, procrastination is something that you are drawn to, but it does not serve you well. Be decisive and move ideas, tasks or goals forward, or make the decision to abandon them – but make a decision. Indecision is stressful and unproductive.

❖ **To avoid boredom, take breaks throughout the day, to walk, exercise or even nap.**

  ▪ You can be a restless beast, so accommodate your desires and take time for scheduled breaks throughout the day. Exercise is especially beneficial, so keep both your mind and body healthy.

❖ **Organize not only your office, but every room in the house (know where everything is).**

  ▪ For people with AD/H, feeling disorganized can lead to stress and feelings of being overwhelmed. Pick one room per week and organize it. This is not a race, it is a journey, so take your time and get your house in order.

❖ **Schedule time to be organized and create a plan, otherwise you will never have the time.**

  ▪ Actually pull out a calendar and plan specific days for organization. If you don't plan for organization, a year will fly by, and you will get nothing done to help improve your quality of life. If you don't take control and plan your life, your life will continue to control you.

❖ **Use a day timer or electronic device to keep track of appointments or time sensitive tasks.**

  ▪ People do not fail as much as systems, so find a good system to help keep you on task. If you are a Microsoft user, you can program Outlook to alert you to appointments or time-sensitive tasks. You can also use your mobile phone, tablet, notebook or any other device that has an application to help make you more organized and time sensitive. You should never have to say "*I forgot.*"

❖ **Don't interrupt people who are talking – let them finish their thoughts before responding.**

▪ This is a system for being a better listener. People with AD/H are so busy thinking about what they are going to say next, that they truly don't listen to the person talking. Try to keep your head empty and open to taking information in. Listen intently, do not interrupt and when the person is through talking, you will know what to say. Listening sends the message that "*I value your opinion.*"

❖ **In your computer, create a "Procedure" file to remember how to perform specific procedures.**

▪ You might create a file folder in your computer titled "Procedures," which is where you store documents that help you remember how to do things that you don't do very often. You might store notes on how to download photos, edit videos, change passwords, pay bills on-line or check traffic on your website. Help yourself remember by documenting some of the tasks you perform.

❖ **Use colored highlight pens to organize and code the importance of certain tasks (for visual people).**

▪ I mentioned earlier in this chapter that I use yellow highlight pens to mark words, sentences or paragraphs that I think are important and that I want to re-read. I also use colored pens in my traveling calendar to highlight birthdays (blue), holidays (orange), appointments (yellow) and warnings or alerts (red). Find a system of color coding that works best for you and add it to your tool kit.

Chapter 10

The Gremlin

Every human being on this planet has an inner saboteur that I call the "Gremlin" and it is relentless in its pursuit of trying to destroy our confidence and self-image. In my previous book titled "**Simple Steps to an Extraordinary Career & Life,**" chapter six in that book is titled "The Inner Saboteur" and it is devoted completely to an in-depth analysis of the Gremlin. For that reason, I am not going to reprint that entire chapter again in this book or rehash all of my previous thoughts. However, I will catch you up to speed, so you understand the concept, but my last book makes an incredible read, so I would encourage you to order that from my website www.BradWorthley.com or in Kindle form through www.Amazon.com.

The word "Gremlin" is basically a metaphor for the internal perceptions, thoughts and feelings we have about ourselves that can disempower us. Perceptions, however, are just beliefs about ourselves to which we develop loyalty. Your Gremlin (yes, you truly do have one) more than likely appeared when you were in school, and it will be with you the rest of your life. It will be with you 24 hours a day and 7 days a week – it never rests in its pursuit of robbing you of your self-worth and confidence. This inner voice can be unforgiving, doubt-producing and energy-draining. It wants to keep you exactly like you are because it hates change. It will constantly remind you of your imperfections, and people with AD/H don't need help in pointing out our imperfections because the education system has been pointing them out to us for years.

Having AD/H may have been one of the reasons you ended up with the Gremlin that you did. Many of you with AD/H (especially the hyperactive ones) may have been disruptive in class, so you put on some serious miles between the classroom and the principal's office getting chastised for your troublesome ways. Some of you should have been given frequent visitor miles for the number of trips you took to have a chat with the principal, who had no idea what to even do with you. It was probably embarrassing to you, which may have created emotional wounds that the Gremlin has used to remind you about throughout your life. Your inner voice may be one that reminds you of how disruptive you are, how you are a distraction to others, unmanageable, difficult, or that you are simply different than other children (making you feel isolated). You might have bought into the Gremlin's story that you are bothersome and an inconvenience to the world. This may be the story that you have developed loyalty to and is repeated throughout your adult life as well.

Chastising a child with AD/H for being hyperactive, or as some people in the education system would label it "disruptive," is like chastising a child who is blind for not being able to read their workbook, a deaf student for not being able to hear the teacher, a dyslexic person for not reading fast enough, or a child with Asperger's for not being a social butterfly. Being chastised is punishment, and punishment should be reserved for when there is ill intent in the child's actions or behaviors. Children with AD/H do not intentionally try to disrupt a class, draw negative attention to themselves or try to get poor grades in school. It is not a "choice;" it is a physical reaction without thought, much like a physical reaction (shaking) for people who have Parkinson's disease.

The disruptive behavior is not a problem; it is a symptom that indicates a child may be struggling with AD/H and not have the tools to manage it. When I say "tools," I mean ones like seeking help from an AD/H coach, medication for some children, adequate diet for other children, or even a diagnosis to help them begin the process to understand their symptoms (and I believe most cases of AD/H are not diagnosed).

Poor grades are not a problem, they are a symptom that the child may have AD/H, and in most cases, it is a lack of retention problem (not a lack of intelligence problem). A lack of attention can cause a lack of retention, so the focus should be on why the child is inattentive. I know many very bright and successful people who said they were so bored in school; they would daydream just to kill the pain of boredom (inattention). Either the class content was of no interest or the teacher presenting the content was boring and not engaging. Either way, some children simply suffer from inattention due to boredom. It has nothing to do with being smart or dumb; their grades are not reflective of their intelligence, only their amount of attention and retention.

Regardless of the cause of the inattention, you are given grades in school that you cannot change (even if it is the teacher's inability to teach well or to fully engage you). They become your permanent record and personal brand, which will define you for many years to come, if not your entire life. People will judge you by your grades whether you are trying to get into certain classes, playing sports in school, trying to get a scholarship, wanting to go to college, seeking a job, or even trying to get affordable auto insurance (many insurance companies give "good student discounts" for good grades). The assumption is that if you get good grades, you must be a responsible, hard working person who deserves recognition for your superior efforts. The funny thing is that the fearless people who started the insurance companies were probably "C" students with AD/H.

You might feel smarter than your grade point average shows, but who is going to believe you? Why should they believe you when it is your word against the entire education system? If beliefs can be quantified, then we tend to accept them as truths; like GPA, SAT, ACT or other tests taken in schools that shape our belief system. Good scores build our confidence and bad scores destroy it. Your Gremlin thrives on bad scores because they give it one more emotional wound with which to remind you for the rest of your life. Sometimes, the questions about whether you are smart or not, which roll around in your head for years, go unanswered.

The problem is; no thought lives rent free in your head. As a person with AD/H (hyperactive in this case) you are always questioning whether you are truly a disruptive force and an inconvenience to others. You are questioning whether you are smart enough to get a good job or have a successful career. You even wonder if you will ever find true love because you question who would want to spend their life with you. There are so many questions rolling around in your head that go unanswered because you have no way to quantify if they are true or not.

I had someone ask me recently at what age I discovered my gifts of AD/H. It was actually in my mid-twenties when I was discovering that I was very creative and capable of some really great ideas. I was able to solve challenges and find innovative solutions in the business world, which is when I realized I had ingenuity. I was always fearless in my sports, but I started to notice that I was also fearless in the business world. I would have friends ask me how I could take such big risks and start so many companies, when they would have been terrified to do such things. I was starting to realize that not everyone was like me and that these gifts were not common to everyone. I was probably around 32 years old when I truly was able to admit to myself that I was unique and that my gifts were real.

The further away I got from my school years and from the grades that defined me, the more confident I became, because I had a new belief system growing. My Gremlin's voice was fading as it tried to continue to convince me that I was not good enough or that my grades proved I was not smart enough. Instead, my own voice was gaining a foothold. The real truths were being told, and I knew them to be true – I was smart and maybe smarter than anyone knew. I could not prove it because I had nothing to quantify it, but I was finally ready to stand up and have a voice about my own gifts, whether I could prove it or not. I struggled with telling anyone how I felt about my unique gifts because it sounded egotistical, and I could not supply proof.

As humans, if we have a lack of information, we fill the space with negative information, even if it is about ourselves. If we can't quantify that we are "smart," or if we have a education system tell us we are not smart enough, then we fill our head with negative stories. They may not even be true, but we tend to go to the dark-side with our thoughts. Then we wonder why depression is one of the biggest challenges with our youth today (that and obesity – are children over-eating to cover the pain of being constantly told that they are not good enough?). Is our grading system, lack of confidence and depression related?

To add insult to injury, sometimes your parents, grandparents, siblings or friends support the Gremlin's story and reinforce it. You bring your report card home, and you are chastised all over again by your parents who are unsympathetic to your challenges. They may be unsympathetic because they are completely unaware of the fact that you may have AD/H. Most parents are completely uneducated about AD/H and aren't even aware if they have it in most cases. Only a tiny percentage of the children in schools are ever evaluated, yet diagnosed for AD/H (somewhere between 3 percent and 7 percent, depending on which expert you ask). Most of the children given consideration for evaluation are the ones who are disruptive because the symptoms stand out, and they are hard for teachers and parents to deal with.

This also brings into question the socioeconomic status challenges with diagnosing AD/H. I am going to assume that most of the children who are diagnosed with AD/H are of a higher economic status. They have parents who have the resources to be able to seek assistance if they see their child struggling. They can afford to hire a psychiatrist, AD/H coach or pay for the medication for their children. Think of how many children get sucked into the same cycle of poverty or economic uncertainty that their parents may suffer from because of their low grades in school and the lack of treatment for the AD/H, which is the cause of the problem. How are we ever going to break that cycle unless every child is given the same opportunity to be diagnosed and treated fairly?

Most children who have AD/H are undetected and are living silently in emotional pain as they have their confidence crushed each day at school. They don't stand out because they are "C" students, which means they are not good students, but they are not bad enough to need attention. They are what I will call the "silent majority" who fall through the cracks and limp through the education system wounded. They escape with a diploma, but no confidence. Undiagnosed, undetected, under the radar screen and emotionally wounded for life – I am just one of those millions of people.

Now add to that the number of children who are "A" and "B" students who also have AD/H and go undetected because neither their grades nor behavior signal a problem. They still suffer with many of the same symptoms as those of us with "C" grades, but they may never get the assistance they need to normalize their life, because the symptoms are not obvious. This is a diagnosis that has no boundaries; it impacts a huge part of our population whether you are rich or poor, male or female, short or tall, black or white.

Sometimes our parents become our Gremlin because of their own inner saboteur. Since AD/H is genetic, they may have their own issues with not feeling "good enough" and may have also been emotionally wounded by the education system's grading methods. If you do poorly in school, they may feel guilty because deep inside, they may know they passed that gene on to you. They want better for you; they push you unreasonably hard, so you end up with a better life than they did. It may be that they perceive your low grades as a direct reflection on their poor parenting skills. There are a number of reasons that our parents can sometimes sound like the inner voice that haunts us, but in most cases, I do not believe there is ill intent; they are just dealing with their own emotional baggage. Going back to my earlier statement, I truly believe it is simply the lack of knowledge surrounding AD/H. If the medical community and mental health community struggle with answers, then you can imagine what a challenge it will be for parents or children.

In the process of writing this book, I have reached out to friends, family, Facebook friends, newsletter subscribers and other people in my community to ask about their experiences with AD/H. I continue to be astounded by how many people are still haunted by their school years, and the Gremlin's voice that reminds them of their pain. The emotional wounds from their school days are still shockingly painful as they remember how they were treated and labeled in school. The emotional wounds were not necessarily from their peers; they were from a education system that labeled and categorized children in an unfair manner. It was a system that seemed archaic in its methods of scoring "smart" and sometimes cruel at best in dealing with some of the symptoms of AD/H. Everything from being locked in closets, sent to the principal's office, being spanked with a wooden paddle, to being berated and humiliated in front of the entire class as punishment. Thank goodness, most of these methods are not allowed in schools today, but some are still being recklessly used out of ignorance. Children are still coming out of our education system with wounds that are invisible to the naked eye.

These wounds are deep, they will be with you the rest of your life, and the best thing to hope for is to be able to manage the pain. The most important thing that you need to know about your Gremlin and its stories is that it lies.

Its stories about you are not true!

The memories you have about actual circumstances and events that occurred in your past may be true, but the meaning that your Gremlin gave them is not true in most cases. The Gremlin has made up stories about you, which are not true, and it uses those stories to control and manipulate you and keep you exactly who you are. It does not want you to change, so it will tell you stories to manipulate your mind.

The Gremlin's primary methodology for controlling you is to instill fear into you and scare you back to conformity and get you to back down from trying new things. The Gremlin will try to mask itself as an ally by trying to convince you that it is actually trying to protect you from emotional pain. But the reality is, it is trying to control, manipulate and threaten you with risks such as:

- *"But, what if you fail?"*

- *"But, what if you are wrong?"*
- *"But, what if you get rejected?"*
- *"But, what if you get embarrassed?"*
- *"But, what if you are not good enough?"*

The Gremlin's voice will try to fill your head with self-doubt with words like "But what if....?," which makes you question yourself. It is normally not a lack of money that keeps people from success; it is a lack of confidence. It makes it very hard to move fearlessly through life, when you have the Gremlin whispering in your ear "But what if.....?" As I have said before, I believe that the biggest risks bring the biggest rewards. But how can you take big risks when you have self-doubt?

My GPA of only 2.47 created a lot of self-doubt in me over my life. I questioned whether I was smart enough to start my own businesses, qualified to be a consultant, write books, create training videos, be a professional speaker and many of the other accomplishments that I have achieved in my life. But that is why I am incredibly thankful for the gift of fearlessness that came along with my AD/H. Even though my low GPA created a lot of my emotional wounds and self-doubt, it was offset with the fearlessness and courage that came along with the diagnoses. It could also be the impulsiveness that comes along with AD/H, which convinces us to push forward with our ideas without much consideration for the potential consequences (that is definitely one of my gifts). Looking back on my fabulous life, I probably would not have done many of the things I have done, if I would have thoroughly analyzed the rewards versus consequences of my decisions. But that is the beauty of me – I am "all in" on a spontaneous and seemingly good ideas – just stand back and watch me go!

I have been able to move fearlessly through life and fend off the Gremlin's voice, because I know it cannot be trusted. I, along with many of my other successful entrepreneur friends, also believe that we may be more tenacious because we have something to prove. Many of my friends are still trying to prove to the education system that it was dead wrong about them not being "smart" or to a parent who did not believe in them. The good news is most of us have already succeeded many times over.

The Gremlin has tried to convince me that I am not "good enough" all of my life, but I know that to be a lie. I have become resistant to its hollow threats as it has continued to try to control and manipulate me with its lies. The voice in my head used to be controlled by the Gremlin as it used to chant "*You're not good enough!*" Today, I control the voice in my head because it is my voice, the voice of my reality. Today the voice in my head is "*I am incredibly smart, and there is nothing I cannot do!*" It is not just a motivational speech or made up story to make me feel better, it is the truth!

Chapter 11

The System is Broken, Not You

I love teachers and have friends who are amazing in their craft as educators, so this book is not an assault on their fabulous profession or even the administrators who are trying to keep the educational system dream alive. At this level, these wonderful people have very little control over the policies or procedures that I believe are so broken. They too are victims of a very broken system. They have no control over the bigger picture – they are paid to administer the wishes of others, whether they agree with it or not.

As an advocate for both teachers and students, I am embarrassed at how little we pay teachers compared to other professions. This is true for most child care professionals – somehow we place very low value on the people who are responsible for our most precious assets – our children. You can work at thousands of jobs that require absolutely no college education and get paid far more than you can as a teacher. It is even hard to be a beginning teacher in a single income home because it is hard to support yourself in some major cities where living expenses are so high (you have to have a significant other or a roommate to help share the expenses).

It is not surprising that 50 percent of the people who enter the teaching profession quit before their fifth year. They are grossly under-paid, under-appreciated and under-supported. They are not given all of the funding or tools needed to be successful, so in many ways, we are setting them up for failure. I truly believe those who come into the teaching profession have their hearts in the right place – it is focused on making a difference in children's lives (it certainly isn't for the high pay or glamorous lifestyle). However, you can only make a difference if you are given the tools to do so and can afford to stay in the profession.

I believe there are a large number of teachers who are good at their craft, but de-motivated by the way they are treated. As mentioned earlier, they are grossly underpaid compared to many other professions with a similar education requirement (nationwide, more than 50 percent have Master's degrees – in the State of Washington, it is 65 percent). They should be paid twice what they currently make, just to deal with some of the overbearing parents and lack of appreciation they endure. They work a lot of hours – not just at school, but most of them also take work home. We don't fund the schools properly, so they are always asked to do more with less. Many teachers buy school supplies with their personal money because they refuse to let money stand in the way of a child's education. I believe that many of these teachers are just worn out and, given the proper resources, could be re-motivated to once again become passionate and perform at a higher level, but we need to find a way to serve their needs first.

If you think back about your favorite teachers, they were passionate and they engaged you. In most cases, we do not train school teachers to do that, or hire teachers because of that skill. Teachers undergo either very little or no training on how to be "powerful and passionate presenters." As a professional speaker, I drive behavior change by being passionate and enthusiastic about my subject matter. It is my job to make sure that my content is relatable to my audiences – the more relatable, the more they retain. I wish the teacher hiring process for the future would focus more on hiring people who are relatable, motivational and have great presentation skills. I am not saying that we don't have these types of teachers in the system now because we do, but it should be required of ALL teachers.

Overall, our traditional public education system rewards retention and recall (or "absorption" and "regurgitation"). This is especially true of the four major core competencies that we are compared to throughout the world, which are reading, writing, math and science. You will be a heralded as one of the chosen few and declared "smart" if you "show up and throw up." In other words, if you show up to class each day, absorb what you are told to, then throw it back up when tested, you are going to be told you are "smart" and rewarded with good grades, scholarships and a college education. But is that truly what smart is? Where are the creativity, ingenuity and fearlessness in that (attributes that you see in the most successful business people)?

Once again, I am not minimizing the achievements of people who get good grades in school; I am still questioning why it is considered to be the primary measure of "smart." Doesn't it seem odd that I have been invited to be a guest speaker, as an internationally renowned business expert, at the University of Washington, but I not be accepted to go there? My grade point of 2.47 would be a great source of entertainment at the admission's office, and my application would be in the circular file (garbage) after the brief laughing fit.

According to the State of Washington Office of Superintendent of Public Instruction, only 2.8 percent of the children in 9th, 10th, 11th and 12th grades are 4.0 students. Out of those, the ones that actually make it to graduation with their 4.0 GPA total 1.4 percent. Didn't you ever wonder why there are so few children in school who can achieve the coveted 4.0 GPA status? I can tell you why, and it goes way back in time.

If you go back about two million years (give or take a year or two) to the day of the Cave people: oops, let me be politically correct and not offend anyone; Neanderthal people: only the physically and mentally superior survived. You had to run fast to get food and if you did not run fast, you became food. Survival required creativity, ingenuity and fearlessness in order to get through each day alive. Wait one minute; aren't those some of the same gifts as many people with AD/H? Well, it all makes sense now – stick with me on this.

Neanderthals with AD/H survived because of their mental cunning and physical prowess. They went on to procreate in large numbers and became successful business Neanderthals who sold condo caves and the first automobiles with stone wheels (I know it is the truth because I watched the Flintstones during most of my childhood).

Unfortunately, the 4.0 GPA Neanderthals that did so well in school; did not do as well in the outside world. They did not have the ingenuity to escape predators and they were too slow for outrunning the prehistoric beasts that would make paté of their fallen prey. Over the years, 4.0 GPA students almost became extinct because of their deficits in creativity, ingenuity and fearlessness, but with new endangered species protection programs put in place by our education systems, they are slowly coming back (but still in small numbers). I wouldn't make this stuff up (oh wait, I am AD/H, yes I would)! In the United States, we have even resorted to importing 4.0 GPA people from other countries just to help bring the GPA population up in our country since we have fallen so far behind the rest of the world in education.

Which brings up the question; do we really want to educate and create more stereotypical 4.0 GPA students who are deficient in some of the most basic survival skills? Are we not setting ourselves up for failure by relying so heavily on this minority to help us change the world? Wouldn't it be smarter, based on the quantifiable history that I just explained to you, to look towards our creative masses for our future? Yes, the creative, ingenious and fearless folks with AD/H. They have proven survival skills, great leadership skills and amazing entrepreneurial prowess. Shouldn't we stop trying to make 4.0 GPA students out of every child (because that will obviously lead to extinction) and look to each person for their natural strengths? The world needs all of our talents, so why can't the education system learn to value each of our unique gifts?

I think that Richard Branson, the founder of the "Virgin Empire," is a great example of someone with the gift of AD/H. Sir Richard Branson, as he is now referred to (he was knighted by Prince Charles in 2000), created a student magazine in 1966 when he was only 16 years old. In 1970, he founded "Virgin" as a mail order record retailer, and shortly afterwards opened a record shop in Oxford Street, London. In 1972, he built a recording studio in Oxfordshire where the first Virgin artist, Mike Oldfield, recorded 'Tubular Bells.' In 1977, Richard signed the Sex Pistols and went on to sign many household names from Culture Club to the Rolling Stones, helping to make Virgin Music one of the top six record companies in the world. With around 200 companies in over 30 countries, the Virgin Group has now expanded into leisure, travel, tourism, mobile, broadband, TV, radio, music festivals, finance and health. Richard Branson is a creative, ingenious and fearless billionaire.

In Richard Branson's new book Like a Virgin: Secrets They Won't Teach You at Business School, he writes *"The simple fact is that formal education and I were never really meant for each other. I suffered from an acute combination of dyslexia and what I suppose would now days would be diagnosed as attention deficit disorder. When I went to Stowe School in the sixties however, I was simply regarded as an inattentive and troublesome student. As a result, I think everyone from the headmaster down was probably relieved when I decided to drop out and pursue my dream (at that time) of publishing my own magazine. Had I pursued my education long enough to learn all the conventional dos and don'ts of starting a business, I often wonder how differently my life and career would have been."*

I mentioned earlier on in the book that I don't think the world is served by having every child be a stereotypical 4.0 GPA student according to today's measurement standards of "smart." The world needs people with all sorts of skills and talents. Once again, who played God and said that only people with a strong ability to retain and recall are smart? As evolved as we are in other areas of technology and science, are we still incapable of admitting that "smart" is more than just a good memory? It is well proven that genetics plays a huge role in both AD/H (poor retention) and being a 4.0 GPA student (superior retention); so does it not seem insane that we are trying to force every child into being something that they are genetically designed not to be? Isn't that truly setting our children up for failure? We have been trying to do this for hundreds of years, and it has not worked, so isn't the definition of insanity to continue to do what you have been doing, but expect better results tomorrow?

There has been a lot of conversation about finding a way to fairly evaluate teachers. I believe that most teachers are accepting of the idea, as long as it is "fair." But how can you measure their performance based on how we measure students today? If the system is incorrectly measuring "smart" in our children, which I believe it is, then how can we hold teachers accountable for the children's performance when we are not measuring the right things? How can you "fairly" measure teacher performance when they have no control over genetics? 22 percent of our children drop out of school and almost 50 percent of the ones that do stay in school are a "C" average or less. Do we really think that this is strictly a teacher problem? It is a systemic problem that teachers have very little control over. I believe it is cruel to measure children on our standards of "smart" today, and it is just as cruel to try to measure teacher performance based on the same standards.

I believe the system we have today for measuring "smart" is going to be viewed in the future as an archaic and barbaric method. We will look back on these times with such tremendous regret about the way we treated children. How we left half of our population with a broken spirit and the feelings of inadequacy. It will get written up in the history books hundreds of years from now as dysfunctional, abusive and grossly antiquated. It will go right along-side the stories, which seemed so right for the times, but so horrendous to us today.

It will fit right in with how, as a nation, we have treated Native Americans and African Americans, by blindly ignoring the many injustices. I cringe at the atrocities we thrust upon them because we accepted it as the right thing to do at the time. Unfair treatment of children will go down in the history books, alongside the way we treated women in America when we did not believe they should have the right to vote. It was not until 1920 that it was ratified and women were finally included in the political process. In the future, the way we scored children on how smart they were, will be discussed in the same classrooms where we are reminiscing about how in 1942 we rounded up 110,000 Japanese

Americans and put them into "War Relocation Camps" against their will. We did it because it seemed to be the right thing to do at the time, even though we did not give consideration to the painful and emotional consequences for those involved. Even today, we are finally recognizing the gay and lesbian community, with many states voting to allow same-sex marriage. We will someday look back on how we treated this segment of American citizens and be ashamed at their treatment as well, but for hundreds of years, we justified it as the right thing to do.

Do you notice a common thread of the examples in the paragraph above; they were all Americans. We are a nation that is supposed to be held to higher standards than the rest of the world and revered for our wisdom, democracy and social consciousness. We chastise many countries, like China, for their lack of democracy and social consciousness, but their children rank higher in education than ours. We keep making decisions that make me question if we really know what we are doing. The horrific decisions that we have made about human life in our past were supposedly made by the "experts" of that time, so maybe we should question today's experts that are making decisions about our children's education and challenging what is really "smart."

In no way would I want to compare, apples to apples, the plight of children in our education system to some of the groups I have mentioned above that have been so wrongly mistreated. I was trying to make the point that in our effort to do what is supposedly right at the time, supposed "experts" have made a whole lot of wrongs, which left a lot of emotional scars. I believe that today, we are sending close to 50 percent of our children out into the world broken from our current traditional public education system, and it seems like we are willing to accept it because "that is the way we have always done it." Many of those groups of people mentioned earlier, that we treated so unfairly in the past, are still trying to recover from the emotional wounds we left them with – a lack of self-confidence is just one. The experts seem to think we should stay the path or maybe tweak the system. I say it is so broken; we need to tear it down and start over. There may be conversations going on about how we can improve our children's grades, but no one seems to be talking about our grading system – which is a huge part of what is killing our children's self-confidence.

In writing this book, I have heard story after story from adults who have AD/H, which was not diagnosed until they were in their 30s, 40s or even 50s (you can read many of their stories at the end of the book). They all have similar stories of being mistreated by the education system, having their self-image crushed, and leaving school with unbearable scars. They are still haunted and embarrassed by the low grades they were given, even though they are successful today. They still hear that voice in their head that tells them they are "not good enough" and most of them are still trying to prove their worth to either the teachers or parents who berated them for their grades. Unless you are one of us, you will never understand the emotional wounds that come along with low grades. That voice of doubt in your head can be unforgiving, doubt-producing and energy-draining and it will be with you the rest of your life.

The education system needs to give more consideration to the radial impact of their decisions and make the right decisions for our children, not the popular ones. However, that is not the way our lawmakers, who have the ability to change the education system, make their decisions. They make their decisions based primarily on their political affiliation, which is why we have such tremendous gridlock in politics today. They can't even agree on how to balance a budget, yet alone tackle something as challenging as improving our education system. I hope there are some politicians that will have the courage to step up and do the right thing for our children and our future. There is nothing more critical, or with such long term annuity, than improving education.

Unfortunately, I could write another entire book on my frustration with this subject as well, but I need to stay focused on this book and this subject (which is very hard for a guy with AD/H). We need to finally admit that the way we score "smart" is wrong, and we need to change our current traditional public education system immediately. I am well aware that this is going to take time, but I am hoping that in my lifetime, we make some major progress.

If I leave any legacy at all on this world, please let it be that this book has a positive impact on everyone's self-image and self-confidence. Not just for the children of our future who are served by the changes in the system, but even for adults today who have never felt "good enough" because they did not get good grades in school. I hope this book allows them to realize that they did have special gifts that served the world, they <u>are</u> truly "smart," in their own way, and the education system was broken – not them. It is never too late to heal.

We know that children with AD/H have an attention problem, which leads to a lack of retention, which leads to lower grades. We also know that many children who are incredibly smart are sometimes bored, so they also lose attention, which creates a lack of retention and sometimes creates lower grades. So, what if we taught all children as if they had AD/H? Inattention is a daily challenge in all schools because not all children are going to enjoy every subject. If all teachers were taught ways to engage students more, encourage learning and entertain them with innovative content, it may keep them active in the learning process and serve everyone. What if all teachers were trained to focus on three goals each and every day (besides curriculum):

- Engage
- Entertain
- Encourage

For many people with AD/H, school was painful because of the blame that occurred and the misdirection of accountability. As an example, the education system gets frustrated with us because we are not getting good grades, so the blame game begins and it is normally pointed at us. *"Why don't you apply yourself?"* or *"You are just lazy"* or *"You need to try harder!"* became the standard dialogue for those of us giving it everything we had but falling short. Did anyone ever consider that it was not us – the close to 50 percent of the population that was not measuring up? Once again, maybe it is the grading system that is measuring the wrong things.

I do not believe that any child goes to school wanting to fail. Every child arrives each day wanting to do well in school and wanting to be praised for their efforts. They want to fit in with everyone else and not be categorized as "disruptive," "unmanageable," or "dumb." They live in fear of being told that they are going to have to be in a "remedial" reading class because they can't keep up with the other children. Or they are notified that because of their low grades, they will be required to attend "special education" classes. What does that do to a child's confidence? Do you think it has an impact on our drop-out rate throughout the country?

In the United States, there are approximately 7,000 students dropping out each school day (March 1, 2010 White House press release). The national average is a little over 7 percent annually, but you have states like California, the nation's largest education system, that have around 18 percent (California Department of Education cited 93,000 dropouts in 2010). According to the U.S. Department of Education, the nation's high school graduation rate is the highest it has been since 1976, at 78 percent, but that still leaves 22 percent still failing to get their diplomas in four years. The 78 percent graduation rate is the total number of freshman students who make it to graduation. Are these drop-outs (22 percent of our children) the outcasts of society and the disruptive ones who don't deserve a good education? Or are they simply regular, everyday children who have been told by the system that they are not smart enough based on how we score "smart?"

Think about it; as a child, you are coming to school every day as requested and trying your hardest to do well, but due to possible undiagnosed learning challenges, like AD/H, you struggle. You are getting failing grades and the teachers are telling you that you are disruptive, unmanageable, and lazy or that you will never graduate. You can't get any special assistance in school, and you are not getting much assistance from home. Your primal fear of "not being good enough" kicks in, because it is now being quantified by people who are supposed to be your advocates. The fear of failure becomes overwhelming (the definition of fear is the anticipation of pain), so you do the only thing you know how to do in order to protect yourself from the emotional trauma of failure, and you drop out. Why go to school every day and be reminded that you are a failure? Are these children "dumb" as the grades lead you to believe, or do they simply have a lack of retention and recall? Is it possible these 7,000 children dropping out each day have some of the gifts of AD/H and are actually very smart? Could they be our entrepreneurs of the future if given the opportunity? Do you know the cost to all of us for having 22 percent of the population unemployable or underemployed?

Research shows that most of these broken souls will end up in our judicial and prison system at some point. The mental health experts will tell you that people with AD/H have a higher than normal chance of suffering from depression, being put in jail or committing suicide. Is it the AD/H that is the cause of these problems or is it the broken traditional public education system that is the cause of these problems? Do children make these desperate choices because they have a "disorder," or is it because they have been repeatedly misjudged by the education system as "not good enough" by a method of scoring that is antiquated and misguided? Is it possible to save these young, precious lives with a new and more accurate scoring system? One that would reward their unique gifts, provide them with hope for the future, and a possible path to success? Or will we continue to let these fabulous young minds suffer in silence?

What if we took the money that we currently spend on unemployment benefits for these people, the cost of our judicial system for prosecuting these people, the cost of keeping them in prisons and all the other social services needed to serve this part of our struggling community and put it into our educational system instead as a proactive approach to solving many of our social ills? I think we would have an abundance of money to do things right, with money left over.

The problem with change is that each state government will hire experts in education to try to solve the problem. But guess who the experts in education will be? The educators! That's right, the stereotypical 4.0 GPA people who flourished under the current system. We will hire them because they must be our best and brightest thinkers – right? Wrong! The current system worked for them and made them look good, so why on earth change it? If it worked for them, then the system can't be broken;

it must be the children that are broken, so let's stay focused on them as the problem. What we really need to do is hire people who are AD/H to come up with the creative, ingenious and fearless solutions that we need to solve this challenging problem. But we won't hire people with AD/H for the job because they will be judged by their lack of qualifications in the world of academia. This is the reason that our traditional public education systems continue to limp down the path of change. Yes, some change is happening, but it is a "Band-Aid," and we need major surgery.

Many children had fabulous experiences and memories from their school years, so I am not categorically speaking for all children; I am speaking about those with AD/H (the ones who are diagnosed and the millions who go undiagnosed). I think it is hard for many people to grasp why poor grades leave such deep and long lasting emotional scars. If you have never had poor grades, it would be hard for you to empathize with people who are AD/H. The interesting thing is that our GPAs become irrelevant in the real world shortly after graduation. As an adult, when was the last time someone asked you about your GPA? My guess is; the age of 23 was the last time most of you were asked about it, and for many people, it may have been the day you were out of high school, which was at 18.

I work with HR professionals throughout the world, and a GPA is pretty insignificant in the hiring process today. They would rather know who paid for your college (you or your parents) to see if you are a participant in your future and whether you have good people skills or not. "Hire the smile and train the skill" has become the new hiring mantra for most customer-facing jobs in many industries. I am not downplaying the need for an education; I am making the point that the current scoring method (GPA) is pretty irrelevant in the real world because the business community already figured out that it isn't necessarily a great indicator of whether someone is actually "smart" or whether they are going to be good at a specific job (depending on the job). So why can't we change the current grading system to a method that makes more sense, and becomes a better indicator and tool for the marketplace. Why can't we create a system that takes all of life's gifts into consideration, not just the ones for people who belong to the lucky sperm club and have great memories?

If our goal is to educate children and prepare them for the world, plus send them off with confidence to become self-sufficient and independent, let's create a system that does that. As of today, we are so far off the mark that it is frightening. As a nation, can we truly be satisfied that 7,000 children are dropping out each day, and of the ones who are graduating, approximately 50 percent have a GPA of less than 2.70 (C average or less)?

AD/H certainly has an effect on our children's ability to learn, but I am not sure our traditional public education system thinks it is a big enough problem to address it. The experts say that between 3 percent and 7 percent of our children have AD/H – I think those numbers are grossly understated. The ones who are diagnosed are only diagnosed because they stand out as disruptive in class. These are the ones who in most cases are dealing with the hyperactivity symptoms of AD/H. These are the children who may get diagnosed and receive special attention because they are driving a teacher or parent crazy. But what about the children like me with AD (attention deficit) who are not hyper, are not disruptive and do not stand out as needing a diagnosis. Our only symptom in many cases is simply low grades, which don't normally demand attention and need a professional diagnosis from a psychiatrist.

It may also not be in the best interest of the traditional public education system to diagnose children with AD/H (or any other learning challenges) because if they do, they may be required by law to provide assistance, which many school districts cannot afford. So how many children will go undiagnosed because of the financial burden to the system if they diagnose children properly? This goes back to my statement of how grossly under-funded our education systems are, and how we are willing to sell our children out in order to save money. Meanwhile, those of us with AD/H just sit in silence and suffer through school and pray we graduate. I believe the number of people with AD/H could be closer to 30 percent of the population. Why do I believe that to be true?

Going back to one of my earlier statements; I do not believe that any child goes to school wanting to fail. Assuming that to be true, why are close to 50 percent of our children graduating with less than a 2.70 GPA, and on top of that, 7,000 children are dropping out of school each day? Were they trying to get poor grades? Did they think it would be fun to fail classes and live with the embarrassment for the rest of their life? I don't think so. I believe most came with good intentions, but suffer from some form of inability to retain what they learned (some of the challenges can also be with English being their second language). Many of those children were not gifted with the genetic predisposition to have good retention and recall; otherwise they probably would have done well in school.

I also believe that around 30 percent of the population has AD/H because of a very unscientific reason. At least 30 percent of the people I personally know (and I know a lot of people), which includes their children, have AD/H. They are a large accumulation of family, friends, co-workers, employees, clients and people I have encountered through my life's journey. Most of those adults were diagnosed only after their children were. I have many friends who are in their 40's and 50's who were just recently diagnosed, and are just going on medications to help with the symptoms of AD/H. It has been undiagnosed or underdiagnosed for so long that I believe the numbers of how many people actually have it would shock the mental health community.

Here are some statistics from the Office of Superintendent of Public Instruction for the State of Washington. The results represent students in grades 9, 10, 11 and 12 in the State of Washington for the school year of 2011/2012. It shows that 44.6 percent of the students have a "C" average or less. Children who dropped out are not included in the following numbers and almost 90 percent of those that dropped out had less than a 2.7 GPA.

Grade Point Average (GPA)		Percentage
Less than 1.0	(E & F)	5.4
1.0 to less than 1.7	(D)	9.8
1.7 to less than 2.7	(C)	29.4
2.7 to less than 3.7	(B)	39.8
3.7 to less than 4.0	(A)	12.8
4.0 or greater	(A)	2.8

I was not able to attain national statistics for the above measures because each state tracks their own measurements. However since Washington State ranks in the top half academically of schools in the 50 states, then the national average for students with a "C" average or less is more than likely greater. You also have to consider how many children drop out due to their low grades (in Washington State, about 90 percent of the drop-outs had less than a 2.7 GPA) and never make it to graduation (nationally, 22 percent of our students drop out before graduating). Our role as parents, teachers and administrators is to build confidence in our children. How can you do that when approximately 50 percent of our children are getting "C" average or worse grades? That is 50 percent of our children leaving school emotionally scarred because of our current grading system.

Good grades are primarily based on a student's ability to retain and recall information (memory, which is primarily genetic), especially in the core classes that we compare our school to the world with:

- Math
- Writing
- Science
- Reading

The big problem is that our current method for grading "smart" is killing our children. It is killing their:

- Dreams
- Careers
- Self-image
- Confidence
- Relationships

It may also actually be literally killing our children since suicide rates among our youths are alarmingly high. The Centers for Disease Control report that it is the third leading cause of death, behind accidents (auto normally) and homicide of people aged 15 to 24. It is also the fourth leading cause of death for children between the ages of 10 and 14. Approximately 5,000 young adults, between the ages of 15 to 24, commit suicide each year. This does not count the thousands who try and do not succeed – those numbers are alarming as well.

Teenagers face the pressures of trying to fit in socially and to perform academically at school. Low grades can certainly create perceptions of low self-worth and low self-image. This may lead many to focus on their failures and weaknesses, instead of their strengths that go unrecognized. This can then lead to depression, the feelings of hopelessness, and pessimism concerning their future prospects. This can sometimes lead to the desire to want to take their lives. According to the University of Texas, 75 percent of those who commit suicide are depressed. Depression can be caused by many factors, like chemical imbalances, or trauma, but the end result is the same. If close to 50 percent of our children (as an estimate) have a "C" average or less, they are certainly at a higher risk of injuring themselves.

Back to my original point: I believe our traditional public education system has the disorder and it is a "grading disorder." There is no need to continue to emotionally punish close to 50 percent of our population with the current grading system. One that tries to convince them that they are not smart enough, not trying hard enough, or not applying themselves, when that is not the truth. When is someone going to wake up and realize that we are setting our children up for failure, which is leaving emotional scars that will last the rest of their lives?

As I stated earlier, the experts say that only 3 to 7 percent of our children have AD/H, however, I believe we have grossly underestimated that number. I believe that upwards of 30 percent of our children may have some inattention challenges. I believe there are numerous reasons this exists but here are just a few of my recommendations for improving our current educational system:

Restructure our education systems:

- **Elementary schools** – continue to teach the basics and evaluate all underperforming children for learning challenges.
- **Middle school or junior high schools** – teach advanced basics, plus more life-skills classes.
- **High schools** – Create education tracks that focus on a broad career path, with classes specific and relatable to their career. Examples of a few tracks might be:
  - Technology
  - Business
  - Mechanical/Engineering
  - Arts (Theater, music, art, photography, dance, etc.)
- **College** – is the advanced technical or graduate school – no additional math, science, English, or foreign language unless it is a necessary requirement of your profession.

Suggestions for improving education:

- Smaller class sizes
- Re-energize "good" teachers
- Increase pay for "great" teachers
- Train all teachers to be powerful presenters
- Score and evaluate teacher performance fairly
- Focus teachers on: Engage – Entertain – Encourage
- Hire future teachers who have emotional intelligence
- Evaluate all children with "C" average or less for AD/H
- Redefine what "smart" is and how we will measure it correctly
- Teach more life-skill classes that are relatable and will serve students in life

- Greater use of technology to do the teaching (the way children learn best)

- Allow children to progress at their own pace, so they don't get bored (not by age)

- Evaluate each student on their different skill sets or innate gifts (like pre-employment testing)

- Hold parents accountable for their children's performance – get them engaged in their child's learning

Education decisions are driven by each state, so all 50 states are going in their own direction and trying to find answers to many of the problems I am talking about. My wish is that all the states could get together and find proven methods to enhance our education system and create some level of consistency throughout the United States that insures success. Bring in successful people from outside the system like Bill Gates and Richard Branson to contribute innovative ideas with "out of the box" thinking (yes, fill the room with people with AD/H). My biggest concern is that we are sending close to 50 percent of our students into the world with a lack of confidence. This is impacting their self-image and self-worth and is creating many challenges for them throughout all areas of their life. We owe it to future generations to figure this out, and do it right this time.

Chapter 12

Be a Perfect You!

I learned a very valuable lesson in authenticity that I would like to share with you. In my first couple of years running Genesis Group, which was my mystery shopping business, I had an encounter that made me conscious of one of my gifts and the benefit of authenticity. I was performing mystery shopping services for a large bank and I was asked by the President of the bank to come to a District Manager's meeting and present some of our findings. This is before I was offering training as one of my services, and at a time when I was pretty terrified of public speaking (like most people).

I stood in front of about 14 District and Regional Managers and presented my findings. I had never been in front of a room full of bankers before, so my narrator was laughing inside at how the entire room of men in black suits and power ties looked like penguins. I was nervous starting out, but about 5 minutes into it, I was on a roll and the fear turned into enthusiasm. I noticed that the more passionate I became about the subject matter, the more they became engaged and passionate about the subject matter as well. The attendees went from leaning back in their chairs with a look of disinterest, to leaning forward, taking notes, smiling and laughing from time to time in appreciation for my sense of humor. The more I let go of the fear and the more I became regular, every day, fun, "Brad," the easier it became and the more they seemed to learn.

When I was through, the President stood up and told everyone he loved the way I presented the information. He liked that I did not try to homogenize the content to make them feel good – I just told them the truth. He asked everyone if they thought it would be a good idea if I presented the same information to all the Branch Managers, so they could learn from the results as well. They all agreed and thought it was a good idea as well.

He asked me if I wanted to take on this project and do the training, and I said I would (even though I had no idea what it would entail, but once again, I am AD/H, so I will worry about the details later). He turned me over to a couple of women in the human resource department who arranged all my seminars for me, and all I had to do was show up and do the presentations.

I arrived at the first location a couple of weeks later and gave the same presentation that I gave to the District Managers. I noticed the two women from human resource, who were sitting in the back of the room, grimacing, talking to each other and taking tons of notes as I spoke. Everyone in the room enjoyed it, and I got a lot of compliments afterwards, which was very gratifying. After everyone left the room, the two women sat me down and told me that we were going to have to make a few changes to the presentation. They told me that these people are professionals in the banking industry, and I needed to professionalize my presentation a little bit.

I had no idea what they were talking about, simply because I had not given it that much thought. I just did what I had done previously, which seemed to work well before. I did not know that I had to speak to bankers differently than other people, but I figured they knew more than me since they had been in banking for many years, so I went along with it. They had me cross things out, add a few things and alter words until it was perfectly crafted for professional bankers.

We went to the second session the next day and the two women sat in the back of the room again, and observed me, as I offered the new presentation that they finely tuned for me. I was not enjoying the seminar because they had me pull the jokes out and the fun content, so it felt very dry to me. It felt more like a lecture, but the women in the back of the room seemed happier this time. They weren't giving me any "stink eye" and their note taking and grimacing was minimal this time. The attendees were polite, but I did not get the great comments afterwards that I had gotten the day before when I did it. After everyone left, the two women from human resource sat me down again, told me it was much better this time, but had me tweak a few more things that they did not like.

Day three, I am getting ready to give my newest presentation to a room full of managers and the President walks in the door. He said he was in town and wanted to introduce me, and he was also excited to see how the managers responded to my presentation. After a brief introduction, I began doing the presentation just like the two women wanted me to. Ten minutes into my presentation, the President of the bank, who was sitting about three feet behind me, reaches up and grabs my suit jacket to get my attention. I turned around and acknowledged him, and he said *"What are you doing?"* I responded and told him I was doing the presentation that I was supposed to do. He said *"Which presentation – because it is not the same one you did for us?"* I told him that I was doing the presentation that the two women from human resource wanted me to do. He said *"Brad, if I wanted them to do it, I would have paid them to do it – I want you to do it your way!"* I tore up the women's notes and went back to being "Brad."

I never have forgotten that story because it was the first time that I thought I might have a great gift, the gift to be unique in the world of training. Be a trainer who had powerful content, was relatable and delivered my message with fun and passion, so all the attendees would enjoy the learning experience. It was from that day forward that I always promised I would work towards being as good a "Brad" as I could become. That includes never trying to be somebody or something I am not. That is the true meaning of authenticity.

The more "Brad" I have become, the more successful I have become. The more I clarify and distill what is important in my life, the better my life has become. My decisions are no longer made by how much money I can make – they are made by how I can serve others best. My last two books are a great example of that.

My last book was titled *Simple Steps to an Extraordinary Career & Life,* and I wrote it not knowing if anyone would buy it because it was not about my normal areas of expertise. At the time I wrote it, I had no vision of it being viable as a customer service or leadership book, I simply knew it was an important message that needed to be written about. Turns out, it has become one of the most powerful and life changing seminars I offer. It is very powerful as a leadership seminar because it gives you a better understanding of how leaders and their employees think and make decisions. It goes into detail about how we are all capable of far more success than we believe we are. However, it also has life changing content that all employees can take home and serve their families with as well.

The book you are reading right now has very little to do with customer service or leadership (even though it would help leaders better understand some of their employees), but it is an important story that I believe needs to be told. It may never become a top selling movie (or will it…..?), but if it validates one adult or child and makes them realize that they are not broken, then the time was well spent. Today, I write for my passion and not for my pension. If I am being authentic and serving the world, the world will serve me as well.

I lived most of my life trying to prove to myself that I was "good enough." I competed in almost every sport you can imagine just to compare myself to others to see if I was "good enough." I even built my dream home at the age of 39 to prove to myself that I was capable of such greatness. But building shrines as a testimony to my greatness was not the answer – it changed nothing about my life. It did not make me happier, and it did not silence the narrator in my head that would constantly question whether I was "good enough." It was when I finally discovered that I was a perfect "Brad," that my life became extraordinary.

I am not trying to imply that I am perfect, because I am far from it. It simply means I have accepted that I will never have a great memory, I will never be a 4.0 student, and I may never understand the "new math." However, I have some wonderful gifts that many people do not have, such as creativity, ingenuity and fearlessness. Those are just a few of the gifts that have made me a perfect "Brad."

When I finally stopped fighting my AD/H and embraced it, life changed. I learned not to fight the inner voice (the narrator in my head), but to listen to it and embrace it. I was no longer going to live a life of embarrassment over my grades from school because I finally figured out that those grades were absolutely wrong. They were a very poor representation of my intelligence. I decided that my grades would never again define me, because they are not who I am, they are just what a broken education system gave me. I was not going to let AD/H define me because that is not who I am, it is just what I have.

Your Gremlin will probably keep whispering in your ear that you are "not smart enough" or "not good enough" for the rest of your life, but it is an absolute lie. You have developed loyalty to a story in your head that was created by the education system. It is not true, but you have been hearing the story in your head for so long that you learned to believe it. It is time to let it go – abandon the lies. You are gifted in so many ways – you are a perfect you!

How does the Gremlin or inner saboteur impact you as an adult? In more ways than I have pages in this book, but some may sound familiar to you. During my days as a single man, I dated women who I perceived as needing me. They were either financially or emotionally in need of someone to take care of them, and that was me. In my head, I believed that if you needed me, then the chance of you leaving me were less. Ironically, most of them left me. That is because unhealthy relationships are many times due to an unhealthy self-image. Sound familiar yet?

I worked in the world of domestic violence as a volunteer for 10 years, where I worked with the children of domestic violence. Women of domestic violence often end up in a cycle of unhealthy relationships where they are abused. As you can imagine, their self-worth is so low because they have not only been physically and sexually abused in many cases, but emotionally abused as well. They have been told by the abusers that they are stupid or ugly and that no one else would want them. They tend to stay in the abusive relationships because they have learned to believe the stories. The abuser is like a Gremlin – spouting lies in an effort to control and manipulate them. The scars from physical wounds will heal, but the emotional scars never heal.

This is why I am so passionate about the need for changes in our traditional public education system. I don't think most people understand how long emotional wounds last. They don't go away with a pill or a few weeks of therapy, they will haunt most people for the rest of their lives. I am fortunate that I have done more than my share of research and education to understand who I truly am and what my gifts to the world are. However, I wish I would have had these answers when I was 18 years old and could have been validated sooner in life. That is why I am writing this book. If I could get the message out to children that school may be a challenge, but your gifts will surface at some point, and when they do, use them to achieve whatever it is you want from life.

The sub-title to this book, "If you don't have it, you should get it!" was done "tongue in cheek," and primarily for comedic effect. I tested the subtitle at a National Publicity Summit in New York, and everyone loved it as part of the title, so I went with it. As I already mentioned, as a child, it may be hard to see the gifts, but as an adult, there are many fabulous characteristics to AD/H that I believe many people would love to have if given a choice. I am talking about the kind of gifts like creativity, ingenuity or fearlessness that are common among people with AD/H. I am fortunate to not have any of the more troublesome co-existing conditions that can accompany the diagnosis (remember, I am pure AD/H), so even though I have been able to embrace AD/H, it may not be everyone's experience.

If my sub-title rubs you the wrong way, or you question whether I truly see my AD/H as a gift, I can offer you the following. Let's just say I found a bottle on the beach, rubbed it, and a magic Genie appeared and offered me three wishes. If one of the Genie's offerings was to make my AD/H go away, I would refuse the wish. If I had the choice of being reborn into the world without the gift of AD/H, I would turn the offer down. Sure there were, and still are times, that it would be nice to have a better memory, but I would never give up the gifts that I have today because they have made me who I am today; a perfect "Brad."

I really do consider myself fortunate, and I love my gifts. I use them to my advantage in the world (play to my strengths) and I have put good systems in place to make up for my deficiencies. Being aware of your strengths and weaknesses is important in the world of AD/H and also in the world of being a great leader of people. It is very hard to be everything to everybody, so be the best "you" you can be!

Chapter 13:

Other People with the Gift

The following are real stories of people with AD/H, which tell of the challenges with the diagnoses, but also offer some of the gifts that they now recognize they possess. The one thing you will notice that is common among most of them is the pain and emotional wounds that come along with the journey through the education system. I used only their first names to protect their identities because many of them are still embarrassed by their grades from school. I want to thank each and every one of the writers for opening themselves up and exploring their past. It was not easy for many of them, so I appreciate their assistance in sharing their journey with all of us. My goal in offering these stories was for readers to put themselves in the shoes of other real people who have AD/H. Each has their own story and each is on a different journey. You may see some of yourself in their stories, and you might even discover that you have AD/H. I believe that awareness brings change, and if you are aware of both the challenges and gifts of AD/H, you will be able to make better decisions for you and your children.

Kelly's Story:

*I discovered my **gift** of ADD in my early adult years. I am positive that my childhood contributed to the development of this creative talent, as I moved every six months, attended over 17 schools from kindergarten through twelfth grade, and experienced more than my share of familial dysfunction! I believe that all of these experiences enhanced my creative gift of ADD, which I now use to manifest a fabulous life each day.*

Now, it hasn't always been an easy road of mastering my mind that races and moves at record speed with more ideas then I can keep up with! In fact, even as I write this piece, my typing cannot "keep up" with the words and ideas that are flowing out.

*As I stepped into my adult life with the responsibilities as a career woman, a wife and a mother of six, I discovered that the multi-tasking that I needed to be successful had actually shifted me into what I like to call… my **gift** of ADD. I perceive my ADD as mastering a mind of creative genius with many windows of opportunities. I envision my mind as a large house with many open windows of thoughts that in turn become creative ideas, and then are eventually put into action. But the challenge I encountered in my early adulthood was a feeling of being overwhelmed by all the ideas that came to me at hyper speed. I did not know how to organize them and harness the creativity of each one of these beautiful thoughts. I also had not shifted my perception to the fact that my creative mind was actually a gift. I truly felt trapped in a house where I couldn't close any of the windows of ideas and thoughts.*

It wasn't until a few years ago that I realized my true gift! I discovered a tool that worked for me to allow my creative process to flow. I was sitting at my computer writing a piece for a publication when I made a choice to surrender to my mind and let it go wherever it needed to. In the past, when I would sit down to put my thoughts on paper, I would make myself just stare at a blank piece of paper until I finished what I had set out to do. This time I allowed my mind to be in charge. Each time I had a thought that had nothing to do with my subject, I would allow my mind to go there for just a minute, and then gently bring it back to the task at hand. Sometimes I would open up my web browser and shop, and then come back to my writing. I wrote a bit more and then I would answer a few emails – then gently bring myself back to my writing. As I surrendered I noticed I had over 30 windows open on my computer! This would probably make other people cringe, but by allowing my mind to "take control" I discovered an opening to creativity. After a few hours, I had written the most beautiful piece of writing I had ever done. This is a tool of mine. You may ask, "How is that a tool?" Well, as my mind moves into a new "room" of ideas and thought patterns, I open another screen. I discovered that when I gave my brain something to distract it for a few minutes, it got out of the way, so my creativity flowed through beautifully and efficiently.

So for those of you that are feeling stuck by the label "ADD" I give this piece of advice: **Get out of your own way, allow your mind to wander and be curious about the creativity that flows within that unfocused, beautifully spontaneous mind of yours! That is the greatest gift you can give yourself!**

Robert's Story:

Attention Deficit Disorder? What's the deficit? Who chose the baseline and determines the deficit? And why is it considered a disorder? Is it just because I do not choose to focus on details, have imaginative ideas, am creative and energetic? Some people have called me lazy or rude because I don't listen long enough to people who ramble on and on who I consider just want to hear themselves talk. I don't pay attention to details of something I don't consider important. I can have multiple conversations going while I work on dangerous equipment. I can easily move on to another task and not worry about the last one. If that's a disorder, I'm sorry for people who don't have it.

I've never chosen to label myself as someone with ADD. I choose not to let someone else's label cause me to judge myself and hold me back from accomplishing all the numerous things I've done. If it takes me more effort to learn a task that others find easier, does that mean I'm handicapped? Maybe, maybe not. Those same people don't accomplish what I do in a day, which probably handicaps them. I chose to put forth the onerous effort to learn to speak, spell, read, do math because they were tools to accomplish my many goals like communicating with those I love or need to work with.

I believe that the label ADD was created, so teachers could separate those kids that don't fit in to the classroom norm. It makes it easier to manage the classroom if they are all drones. The kids with the ADD label don't like to sit for hours in a little box called a desk and memorize things that they don't feel will benefit them. My mind can't stop daydreaming if it's still for 25 or 30 seconds. I'm never bored. By the time the teacher was done with a five-minute lecture, I'd already been thinking circles around the subject and unfortunately I only got about every other word. So I became the class clown to take the attention off myself and to try to entertain the teacher and make friends with them just so they would give me a passing grade.

Some people with ADD have been diagnosed as depressed, which surprises me because people with ADD tend to look outward and focus on external circumstances rather than on themselves because their own psyche bores them. There's not enough action in their own lives to entertain them, so they look for it elsewhere … or they create it. Perhaps they seem depressed because other people are telling them that they are not good enough the way they were created.

So many geniuses from the past must have had ADD the way they were described by historians. Maybe they did. If they were alive today, we would say they were rude or crazy and can't focus on one thing at a time ... and then try to medicate the behavior. Imagine what we would have lost if Mozart had been medicated. All those people who tried to hold me back and shamed me into thinking I was mentally handicapped. I'd like to meet them now and show them what a success I am. If they would have held me back, put me in a "special class" or medicated me, I would not be the success I am today.

I am married to a great woman who is on the other end of the spectrum: very detailed and focused. Together we make a hell of a team, but it's because we choose to work at it. I have to slow down and talk about one subject at a time and finish my thoughts. She has to interpret what I'm saying and put it into the subjects where they belong. I have the ideas, and she figures out how to make them work. Then we work alongside each other to make them happen. For instance, when we bought our house, we moved my mother-in-law in with us and two months later began to add 20 feet on to the house, remodel the kitchen, put in three patios, build a 140-square-foot gazebo, all from August to the next January. Since that short time ago, we've traveled to other countries, built a classic car from the shell up, bought and sold other properties, and begun two more businesses. Life is too short, and we choose to embrace this "disorder" they call ADD.

Matt's story:

"Scatterbrained, but lovable," is how I was described by a coworker, two days ago. This, from my employer during a recent performance evaluation: "Your personality is tremendous, and you're obviously very intelligent, but you need to become more consistent with your production and quality of work." If I had to venture a guess, these exact words have come from the mouths of perhaps two dozen

teachers, seemingly innumerable counselors, my parents, and most of my previous employers. I nodded to my boss, delivered the response I used hundreds of times to the dozens of people before her. "I know. I'll work on it."

For me, living with ADD has truly been life-long. Ask anyone who knows me, and they'll tell you they knew I had it from Day One. My earliest memories are of being anywhere but the present, constantly creating new worlds with toys, illustrated books, nature. My mind was never in one place at the same time, and my body was not long to follow, which made the rigors of school extremely difficult, from onset to completion. Had it not been for a young diagnosis, an onslaught of medication, and countless generous accommodations by the public education system (and subsequent colleges), I have no clue where I would be today.

Instead, I graduated high school on time and earned my Bachelor's degree in five years and one quarter (Go CWU Wildcats!). I overcame the disorder, with lots of help. However, while I survived academia, I'm learning that things are different in adulthood. The accommodations are becoming less frequent. In adulthood, concentration is not merely a function, it's a virtue.

At 27 years of age, my thoughts continue to wander far and wide. Conversing with me requires a high level of patience, as you may have to repeat yourself several times (thank God I have a patient girlfriend). One minute I'm writing this essay, the next, I'm pondering a book I read last week, or recalling elements of a conversation held the day before, or becoming angered about something from months ago; then, because I'm lucky, all of those things at once. I could be completing a task at my job when the allure of my iPhone calls to me all the way from inside my desk drawer. It's saying, "Check the score of the Seahawks game. Check Twitter. Hey, maybe it's your turn on Words with Friends." My iPhone is very persuasive.

Regardless, I have not medicated for ADD since I was 23. This was a conscious decision, as I felt meds blotted my creativity and swung my mood to vast extremes, as I believe focus is easier to control than mood.

I graduated college with a degree in creative writing, which I use to write and publish short stories and poems, perfect forms for me: they can be as short as my attention span allows them to be, but, with persistent revising, are capable of utmost potency. I've also written articles and columns for music websites, literary blogs, and other places. When I set aside time for myself to write, and utilize that time, it stabilizes me throughout the day. The ability to create new worlds on the page has no doubt aided me in the real world. Through dysfunction, I found my passion.

Balance remains difficult to achieve — particularly in the workplace and with personal interactions — but as long as I have time to write, as long as my girlfriend continues tolerating me, as long as I hold down a job, I have no desire to change who I am. I am a perfect Matt Robinson - I am proud of who I am. Who else would I be?

Terry's story:

As a child in school, I could not sit still. I was squirming in my chair, tapping my pencil, tying my shoes repeatedly, or doing anything involving movement. I was not intentionally trying to be constantly moving or to be disruptive; I just could not control it. I struggled with school, especially writing, because grammar was a real challenge and still is to this day. The worst thing you could ask me to do is write - I feel tortured by the process to this very day. I did pretty well in math as long as it was about memorizing formulas, graphs, matrixes or anything else visual. However, if you moved the numbers around or changed the visual, then I did poorly.

Many of the challenges with growing up with ADHD were time and priority issues. I would not get my homework done on time because I would procrastinate. It wasn't necessarily the difficulty of the work (unless it was writing), it was just starting the work, but once I got started, I was fine. I was told repeatedly by my father that I was not applying myself, so the lack of empathy or understanding for my struggles was hard on me.

I found out I was ADHD when I was 45 years old, when my two sons were diagnosed with it. I was listening to the Psychiatrist talk about my son's challenges with ADHD, and that is when I realized they were my struggles as well. I have just begun taking Adderall in an effort to control some of the negative symptoms. I survived school because I was very outgoing and charismatic. I graduated with a 2.8 GPA, but I can admit that it probably should have been lower than that, but teachers loved me, and I believe gave me many breaks because of my charming personality.

One of the positive side effects of the ADHD has been my fearlessness. In high school, I used to ask the most popular girls out on dates because I was not afraid to do so. I was not afraid to try out for sports because I was fearless. I have been extremely good at sales all of my life. Fearlessness has made me one of the top sales performers in most of the companies I have worked for. I'm not afraid to pick up the phone and call anybody – I normally go after the top dog and work my way down. When I get someone to listen, I'm very creative and have fun finding solutions. Being ADD makes me very competitive – I hate to lose and want to be best at whatever I do. I am good at making friends and building relationships, and I give ADHD the credit for that valuable gift (the gift of "gab").

I believe I am very street smart, even though I was not very book smart. I have the ability to solve problems and find solutions that others have not been able to. Add that to the fearlessness of not being afraid to test new ideas and try new concepts, and those attributes are very valuable in the business world. I am very well organized most of the time, because it brings order to my life. It is a good system, which helps keep me less stressed. When I put my mind to something, I can become hyper-focused and get a lot done. Even though ADHD has its share of challenges, the gifts have made me who I am today. Now that I have been diagnosed and am able to understand what I am dealing with, it helped make many things about my life clearer. The biggest thing I am clear about is, my grades in school were not who I was, they were just what I had. I am smarter and more street wise than those grades gave me credit for.

Sharon's story:

When I was a child in Catholic elementary school, I simply could NOT sit still in my chair. This was somewhat of a joke with the nuns. However, I came up with a solution that worked for them and me. I would have my desk be at the end of the row (which sometimes did create more problems with attention) just so I could have one knee on my seat and have the other leg standing on the floor. This was done just to manage my feelings of having to move and not be standing in front of a row of other students who could sit still.

And in third grade, my teacher was so creative; she decided that she would tie me to my chair since it was so hard to get me to sit still. Actually it seemed like a joke at the time, and she never really had me do it for long. She was acutely aware of the fact that I wasn›t able to sit still, period.

To this day, I cringe when I hear parents and teachers say.... "what's wrong with you...sit still...what's your problem? as if the children are "defective." Is the understanding that "good children sit still?".... It's so unfair for all of those sweet, creative, souls to be made to feel inadequate because "they" cannot conform to the restrictions that some classroom situations require. Physically moving one's body increases the ability to focus, and I believe it is an effective learning strategy for many children and adults with ADHD

For me, there certainly were subjects that simply didn'*t hold my attention. I was bored. So that meant I would have to just memorize the content in order to pass the tests and move on. Not an easy task. To some extent I was successful. If I was actually interested, I could spend hours reading about something, but that was rare in the first 12 years of school. I did manage to figure out that in order to retain any of the knowledge/reading materials, I had to be in a **very** quiet environment, or at least an environment with enough "white noise" that I wouldn't get distracted.......Going to a library was an inside joke for me. Seriously there were too many distractions there to read!!*

*It was that I would pay **too much attention** to things going on around me. The difficulty for me came from trying to "filter" out all of the stimulus/noise/lawnmower/pencil tapping/nose sniffling/paper turning NOISES. I would be shifting and maintaining attention on one thing then would be pulled in so many directions with all of my thoughts and the activities and sounds going on around me. This trait can be a liability in some environments (like school), and can be a gift in other environments (as a doctor in an emergency room, entertainer, inventor, nurse, police officer, etc.). I have found with time that my intuition is more acutely tuned in to physical behavior, verbal and nonverbal.*

Other descriptors from being ADHD.....to some extent I am a non-conformist. I have thrived under conditions that could be considered chaotic. Raised four boys, and you can imagine what my friends thought of that household. I had an organized and clean house most of the time....really the only way I could have survived THAT chaos......smile. My husband at that time, worked long hours so I was cook, housekeeper, chauffeur, teacher, event planner, necessity shopper, counselor, nurse, a Black Belt in Taekwondo, with three out of the four boys Black Belts as well. We thrived under pressure. The harder I would work, the "clearer" my mind would get. I was never diagnosed as a child; however, I was diagnosed later in life when working with a Psychiatrist regarding issues with the children.

Judy's story:

I struggled in school, so badly. I have no idea what my grade point was, but I am sure it was barely passing. I didn't care or want to know because I knew it was bad, and it is embarrassing to this very day to even think about it. My husband has asked me what it was; I have told him I do not know.

Besides being teased by other kids as a child for being ugly and having braces, probably my most vivid memory of bad grades was when, with much encouragement from my school-mates, I decided to try out for cheerleader. After all, that was THE most prestigious honor at the time, and perhaps if I won, I would finally gain a little respect from some of the kids instead of being teased.

Well, that was short-lived, when after 2 weeks of rehearsals, right in the middle of a rehearsal; I was called into a counselor's office and told that I could no longer continue with tryouts or rehearsals "because my grades were too poor!" They also told me that I would never be able to go to college because my grades were so bad. I could have died a thousand deaths that day. I lied and told the girls at tryouts that I had changed my mind. Even though that was a long time ago, it was pretty difficult for a young teenage girl to face the fact she was too stupid to even try out for cheerleader.

Oh well...ancient history...there were lots of things that happened back then that I sure didn't understand at the time, but unfortunately, we tend to blame ourselves or that we just were not good enough. I unfortunately, went through most of my life feeling just a little stupid some of the time! I refuse to open up old wounds because they just make you dig too deep and make one feel bad... so I just chalk it up to growing up and that crazy thing called "life."

As far as strengths...probably my best quality and the first thing that comes to mind is my organizational skills and my attention to detail (I am a good proof reader). I am also very well disciplined and I always set out to do the right thing with everything I do. I believe I am very intuitive in reading people (as to their personality) and I am a hard worker who gives great commitment to the job at hand. I am a social butterfly, very outgoing and love to entertain in our home. I also enjoy a very artistic side and have a good eye for photographing (my niche is photographing unique doors and windows).

Kevin's Story:

I was diagnosed with ADD and dyslexia as a child and my teachers would tell my parents that I was "artistic," and will be just fine. I struggled horribly with academics in school, but I flourished socially. No matter how hard I studied, I would only get "C" and "D" grades, so I eventually just stopped trying and only did the amount of work needed to pass. To me, a grade of "A" or "D" were the same thing – passing, which is all I cared about. I had a very hard time focusing in class because the teacher would be talking, but I would be thinking about girls or other things that interested me more. I ended up in summer school a few times in order to make-up classes that I failed. I smoked marijuana quite a bit in my school days, which was probably a form of self-medication in those days.

One of the gifts that I had very early on was one of being very outgoing and charismatic. Most of my teachers enjoyed me because of my personality and I used that to my advantage to survive in their classes. Looking back at it, I used to use my charm as a tool to manipulate them and turn them into advocates for me and my cause to graduate. My teachers knew I was not "book smart," but they knew I was "street smart," so many of them gave me passing grades just to keep me moving through the system. Even though

I struggled with school, I was a good athlete, sang in a rock band and did very well with girls, so I did have a fair amount of confidence, but it was from things other than academics. They let me graduate five credits short of the requirement and with a 2.13 grade point average.

As an adult, I have been incredibly successful and people that have known me for a long time wonder how. I have always done extremely well in any job that required relationship building. I knew I had the gift of charisma, and I used that gift in business and my social life. One of my earlier jobs out of school was working as an insurance salesperson. I was the top money earner, and I won almost every sales award there was to earn. I was eventually fired because my spelling was so bad, but I knew I had a talent and would be successful. I was driven to prove to people that I was better than my grades made me out to be. I was driven by my own expectations of wealth and happiness, not by what others thought. It is my own confidence in "me" that has propelled me to an incredibly successful business that I created from nothing. It has also given me a great personal life with all the toys and money I need, as well as great family and friends.

One advantage of being Dyslexic and ADD is I can read contracts across the table from me, upside down and backwards as fast as right side up. Truly humorous when negotiating deals when the adversary on the other side of the table realizes what I am doing. At that point, they feel threatened, and might as well be a limping gazelle. If I had to choose words that define the gifts of ADD for me (my wife contributed as well), they would be cunning, social, self-assured, compassionate, emboldened, driven and persistent.

Heath's Story:

I am 42 years old now, and back when I was in school there was nothing called ADD, I was simply labeled a troubled kid. It all started in middle school where I always got in trouble for talking.

I even once got put in a closet for my talkative ways, but did it stop me from talking? No it did not.

Through my high school years, I was kicked out of most of my classes for disrupting the teachers. I thank God for some "behind the scene" teachers who went to bat for me and helped me out. They pulled strings and got me in other classes that fit me better, so I would not get further into trouble.

I even had to sign contracts that I would not talk in class, but the school structure was not meant for people with ADD, and I broke contracts. I was not a troubled kid in all areas of my life; it was just in school. I even had a teacher say I needed psychiatric help; however, that teacher was actually fired for that. I did graduate from high school but not with a very high GPA.

Now I am a successful manager/leader for a medium size retail company and a Godly leader in the Christian community. Today, my ADD has evolved into the gifts of creativity and fearlessness, which is complimented by very high integrity. It also gave me a gift of being good at multitasking, which helps me get my varied workloads done in a timely manner. I am very confident in who I am now and very confident in my ability to teach and lead people. I study a lot about leadership and dealing with people. I never liked to read in school, but now I love reading and have a library of more than 1,500 books.

Jay's Story:

This is about my life with an ADD son. Matt started his life differently than anyone we knew. He survived a head on car accident when he was still in the womb at 8-months gestation. After two days in the hospital, the scare was over and he was born a beautiful boy. We followed up at Children's Hospital for months until he was given a clean bill of health. Thank God, but it didn't guarantee he would be different.

Even at an early age we noticed how fixated he was on any one of a number of things; dinosaurs, pirates, alligators, snakes, vacuum cleaners, and many other things. (Yes, I said vacuum cleaners.) We didn't live in a neighborhood with a lot of kids, but as we socialized with other parents and their kids, we noticed we could have a conversation with the kids without ending the first or second question with "Do you know how much a killer whale weighs?" or "How long is a crocodile?" or "Do you know how big a T-Rex's teeth are?" Well son, I just wanted to know if you'd like a hot dog or a burger patty. Welcome to our life.

He was so sweet and outgoing as a kid, but somewhere around the 3rd grade, he noticed he was different, and literally overnight he became very quiet in social settings and much more thoughtful about what he said and when. Maybe he was teased in school, or we asked him once too many times to try and stay on task to no avail, but regardless he changed.

School was so very challenging for him, but he not only graduated from high school, but college, with a slow start, but finishing with a bang. Each year his grades got better and better, and once he was old enough to make his own decisions about meds, he chose to be free of them and express himself in the "light of day." We were very proud, just concerned that a life without the additional focus the meds gave him would make his journey through school too much for him.

What I never saw coming was the Mariner's 116 game season. Sports have always been my thing, but Matt was never much into them, either playing or watching. Well the M's changed all that for him and for me. Don't let anyone tell you that ADD kids aren't smart. My son could read when he was three (I think earlier but don't want to brag) and could recite all the presidents in order by the time he was 5. So memorizing all the statistics of the M's was hardly a challenge at the ripe old age of 18. Oh, I have to add all the stats of every pro basketball team, historical stats of all major sports, draft picks and the order they were drafted in, batting and pitching stats, QB ratings, and more. He's the stuff movies are made of and overnight I had a sports fanatic. No matter what else we disagreed on or saw in different ways as he grew older and did his job to separate from his parents…we had sports and still do. It has been the tie that binds and will always be there for us as well as so many other things we connect on.

I thank God every day for who my son is and the passion he feels for the things that are important in his life. He lives for his passions and not just what his Mommy and Daddy and society want for him. Sure he'll have to move in the direction of security to raise a family someday, but it will be when it's his turn in the box (a sports metaphor!).

Daren's Story

I guess I have never really related my ADHD to being an attribute or a disorder. My only exposure to it as a disorder was as a young kid because I was extremely hyperactive and drove my brothers & sister crazy because I was a pest and a wild child. I was always moving and could not sit still. It wasn't like I had a choice, or gave it any thought, I was just very active. Then I guess the solution was to give me Ritalin when I was about 8 or 9 years old, since our Dad was a Pharmaceutical representative. It made me all mellow, and I kind of stayed pretty much that way through school.

I never have known (or thought about) if I had ADHD anymore as an adult, but my 33-year career as a successful chef put me in a totally turbulent world where chaos is standard operating procedure. Your mind races, and it is about reacting, instincts and reflexes and doesn't have much to do with linear thinking. When I did more administrative roles, I was not good at sitting for long periods or constant paperwork, although I got a lot done and was pretty good at it.

So I guess when I ask myself if I still have ADHD, I shrug my shoulders not knowing – I guess we all have it a little bit. I find myself being reasonably excited about owning my own retail store now, and I have a kind of disjointed work approach. I'll work on about five or ten projects and do them all kind of simultaneously. I will do stuff like labeling items, pricing products, filling orders, cutting a check or two, looking up stuff online, check e-mail and Facebook. At the same time I am also getting a lot of distractions from talkative guests as well. I enjoy the social interactions with people, which makes retail fun for me.

I just bounce in a circle eventually putting a bow on most stuff by days end. Even though I have not taken Ritalin since I was a child, you might say I have been self-medicating with decades of liberal pot use, and I am a pretty moderate drinker. My main goal is to be happy all the time, with just a tiny bit of contrast to remind me of why it feels good to be happy all the time!

Shawn's Story

I believe that I am ADD because my young son was diagnosed with it, and I have all the same symptoms. I think that in today's world it is more helpful than hurtful. Today it is more important than ever to multitask. With so many ways to communicate now, you have to be able to switch gears quickly. Many times in a day I need to stop typing an email to pick up the phone, text someone back, or talk to someone in person that walks into my office. Also with Skype, IM, Facebook, Twitter, etc… there is a lot flying at busy people on a lot of different platforms and bouncing from platform to platform is key. There are times where I have my laptop open working when a text pops up on my phone and I'm Skyping on my tablet.

Even though I had many of the same challenges that my son is having with school, I have found ways to adapt as an adult. I have had many great opportunities in my life because of some of the gifts that I believe ADD has given me. I am very outgoing and good at building friendships and business relationships, which has served me well. I have risen to the ranks of sales manager for a very large distribution company at a young age, which has required my people skills and ability to adapt to many situations (the creative side).

The world is moving towards feeding the multitasking person. If you watch news or sports channels, that is exactly what is happening. There is a ticker going across the bottom of the screen, different information at the top of the screen along with an Anchor giving yet again something different. There is also more interactive TV where shows want you to log on to your tablet or computer or use your phone to participate in a live online vote while the live TV show is playing.

Life is about turning challenges into positives, and that is what I think ADD is. My son has it, but I don't want to medicate it because I know later in life he is going to be able to use it to his benefit. Teachers get frustrated when he and other kids have a tough time focusing on the task at hand. Yes, there are certainly times where it is important to focus all of your attention on one meeting, project, or person. I think that it is turning into the exception and not the rule.

Jennifer's Story

I've tried to recall if I have had ADD/ADHD my entire life or just as an adult. When I think about my childhood I can never remember having too much energy or being disrespectful or out of control in any way. However, I wasn't raised with the opportunity to be any of those things. I grew up on a farm where I was expected to participate in daily chores, which were not only responsibilities but actual physical hard work. After hours of that, all of my left over energy was spent running, playing and sweeping out my play house, which I did several times a day. I was pretty much an average student. I listened in class but felt bored most of the time and rarely did homework until the period before it was due. Somehow I managed to make it through high school with about a 3.8 GPA and was then launched into the "real world."

It wasn't until I was in my late thirties, had owned my own business since the age of 22 and was currently managing twenty some employees and my own household before anyone ever mentioned to me that I had ADD. It was first pointed out by my staff who noticed that I would start several projects or little jobs at a time and never finish any of them until all of them were in full swing. My brain never turns off. I create in my sleep, I create in the shower; I create while I'm creating. Watching a movie is hard. I can think of many other things while I am doing that and multi-tasking is as familiar to me as my own face.

The first time I ever saw what "I" considered to be ADD was when my daughter invited a friend for a sleep over one night. The girls were very excited to watch the latest movie that had come out on video so I got it for them, and we all proceeded to watch it. About fifteen minutes into the movie, the little girl was no longer on the couch watching the movie, she was currently rolling back and forth on the floor as fast as she could and taking little breaks between rolls to make comments on the movie. This was astonishing to me. How could she not be glued to the movie she so badly wanted to see? I personally thought it might have something to do with the huge bag of Skittles candy her mother had sent over with her, so I made the suggestion to her mother the next day that perhaps her daughter had sensitivity to the food dyes in the candy and told her about her behavior. She said her daughter had what was called ADHD, and she needed the Skittles on a daily basis, and what I should have done was given the little girl some coffee. What? So that was how I was introduced to ADD or ADHD.

As an adult with ADD I often confuse what is "normal" with what is actually a symptom of this disorder. For instance, one of my biggest battles is constantly being late. I always think there is just one more thing I can get done before I need to leave. Or feeling very overwhelmed because I have jam packed my life with so many projects I don't know how I will ever get it all done but I do this all by choice, so I never thought that it could actually "not" be my choice.

Realizing there was a diagnosis for this behavior didn't make me feel better, but it did help me to understand it and realize I am not alone, and that I could make choices in my life in order to overcome this, just like someone would if they had any other disease or disorder. If you have diabetes, you might be a diabetic for the rest of your life but you have choices in how you manage that disease. And so it is with ADD/ADHD. I had been doing this my entire adult life and so to have a name for it gave me perspective and power in how it affects my life.

The draw backs to being ADD/ADHD would be that I really never stop. I find that I do not know how to relax like what I would consider "normal" people do. I'm constantly "on". My brain is going all the time, and I am always creating something mentally or physically. Sometimes I am embarrassed of my behavior in front of other people when it seems like I make a bigger mess than was already there before I bring it all together and create a masterpiece. This is all normal to me. It seems like a distracted disaster to other people or that I can't focus, but it's how I function. Having too many balls in the air and not knowing how to prioritize them is simply a way of life for me.

The pros for this type of behavior would be something like this. When my energy is focused towards good things, which is pretty much most of the time since I do consider myself to be a responsible adult, I think I am more successful and more driven than most people. I believe my ability to "not concentrate" or having "hyper energy" has led me to be a successful business owner as well as many other things I have done in my life, which I consider to be good and worthwhile. Is this a disorder? If so, maybe we all should have a little more of it.

Kasey's Story

I was not diagnosed until I was an adult. My boss of 20 years read an article that he said described me to a tee. I read the article, took an online test that confirmed his thoughts and then off I went to see a doctor. I took medication for about six months but decided I had created a world where my ADD served me well. I needed to be able to juggle multiple tasks and keep my big picture perspective. The medicine gave me laser focus, but I would get oddly irritated at interruptions. At the time, I was managing a large real estate portfolio and I knew the interruptions were not going to stop so the medicine had to go.

I am the fourth child of eight. I have a brother who is a year older than me whose ADD was more progressed than my own; he was labeled hyper-active. The two of us were always on adventures, and lucky for us we grew up in a time when kids could be outside unsupervised for hours. I cannot imagine the chaos we would have caused if we were to have had a more restrictive environment. School was a bit more challenging, I was terribly shy, and I had a teacher once put me in a special education class because he did not believe I was grasping math concepts. A month after being in this class, the special education teacher moved me to an advanced math class, and in my fourth-grade year, I finished high school level algebra. Thank goodness for teachers who recognize intelligence outside of the norm. We rarely worked from a book, but problem-solved real life situations. I did well in her class and others where I did not have to work strictly in a lecture-book situation. I remember my teacher telling me my brain worked a little different than others, and she thought I had a beautiful brain. I came to her class ashamed and left proud of my "beautiful brain."

Most of my experience with ADD has been positive. My father always seemed to understand that people learn and create differently. I think we were an active family, and all very athletic. This gave us an outlet that was much needed. My parents never saw our hyperactivity as wrong, so I never considered it a deficit or even recognize it as a disorder.

As an adult, I was drawn to a career where I had to have many plates spinning at once. I love the chaos and stress of a deadline-driven life. I have always recognized my weakness. I will never be a detail person. Small tasks have always escaped me, so I have always hired a detail person to work with me. This person is generally the polar opposite of me and someone that I am sure I drive absolutely crazy! Because let me tell you, I cannot live without this person, but detail-oriented people drive me nuts!

I have learned over the years that I am an action person. I never spend a lot of time in planning stages, I see a course of action, and I go for it. For the most part it has served me well. I am able to problem-solve quickly and I act accordingly. This is one of my strongest assets as an employee and leader. This has gotten me in trouble romantically, but we can't have it all, can we?

I have taken college courses later in life, and small things helped me to sit through two hour lectures. I observe teachers before I take their course and try to only have professors who I find engaging. I sit in the back of the room, so if I need to stand, I can, without disturbing too many people. I can't describe the anxiety of not being able to move. It's like having a sudden desire to shed one's skin. I have done much better in college than I did in high school. I was a very average, if not a poor student in high school. I have often said I did not learn anything in school after the eighth grade – until college.

I do have to admit that sleep evades me. My brain does not shut off like most people. I sleep four-to-six hours a night at the most. My father and brother also have an inability to shut down their brain at night. I often wish for a power button.

Renae's Story

I have been told I have ADD most of my adult life. Not from any doctors or professionals, but friends and family who know me very well. It used to really bother me because the term made me sound broken, and I would defend myself and say, "I DO NOT" But in the past three to four years, some of the most successful people I know have been actually diagnosed with ADD. I started noticing I had a lot of their same traits when it came to business and my household. I finally have come to the realization that I DO have ADD......and you know what? It's not so bad.

I own two real estate offices, I have a husband that has a very high profile job that requires a lot of his time, and three teenagers living at home, plus I'm on several boards for community organizations. People are constantly asking me, "How do you do it? You are always on the go and involved with everything?" I honestly have to say, I don't know. I do know that I can multi-task better than most and that my mind races late in the evenings with fabulous and innovative ideas.

Now, controlling the ADD is a challenge from time to time. For example, multi-tasking can push me off the deep end if I don't keep myself focused on each task (I know, focused and ADD normally don't go together). Also, I am learning to keep some type of writing devise next to the bed in order to keep notes on my creative thoughts. If I don't write them down, I will either forget or lay awake trying to remember them, so draining my brain is important (Thank Steve Jobs for the iPhone!).

With all this said; would I prefer to not be ADD? No, because it is who I am, and I honestly don't believe I would be where I am today without the gift of ADD.

John's Story

I have ADD and I am proud of it! I never knew I had ADD until I was an adult. I would hear about all these kids nowadays that have ADD, and I wondered if there was something wrong with the water. I finally learned about some of the characteristics of ADD and realized I had most of them myself. I'm glad I didn't learn that I had it as a kid because I thought I had enough problems as it was.

I enjoyed the social aspects of school, hanging out with other children my age and having fun. When it came to sitting still in a classroom – that is where I struggled. I just couldn't seem to stay interested in all the things they taught in school. When most teachers spoke I was tuned out thinking about other things. It's not that I didn't try sometimes, but all I knew is that there was a lot of struggle involved when it came to concentrating on any one thing. I didn't feel that I was stupid, but I didn't feel that smart either. I ended up scraping by in grade school and never did finish high school. I did, however, get my GED after joining the U.S. Army.

Now I am 48 years old with no college degree. I know that I am not school educated, but I ended up doing ok for myself. I spent most of my adult life working in the construction industry. Seven years out in the field doing hands-on construction work and ten years in management. I moved up the ladder at a decent pace because of my expert construction knowledge and my abilities to effectively train others. Today, I am a senior project manager making well over $100K and have a growing start up business on the side that fulfills many of my core passions.

Some people ask me if I regret having not received a college degree, and I tell them that I don't regret it all. I possess the equivalent of multiple degrees now simply from years and years of experiential learning, training others and continuously driving myself to gain knowledge any way that I can.

When I think back, I wonder what life would have been like if I would have been recognized for my strengths when I was a kid rather than being graded on a benchmarking system that is unrelated to life. Why am I proud of having ADD? Because if I didn't have it, I wouldn't be the person I am today – a deep intuitive thinker with a highly creative mind that drives towards the simplification of life for myself and others.

Nem's Story

I just turned 40 and have battled lots of "unexplainable" worries, moods, etc. They have been mild but I've dealt with them all my life. I've been on anti-depressants since I was 16....but still...the feelings never subsided. The years and years of drug trials, etc. really messed with me. (My poor husband – he's been amazing). While in the meantime, I was running a successful business, raising 2 amazing boys, and keeping myself very involved & "celebrified" in the community.

Then my life changed; just recently my doctor (love her) looked at me and said chuckling (while I talked about all the new changes in my life, my new puppies, showing pictures on my phone at the same time, oh, look shiny ball...etc. etc.) "I've been your doctor for a year now...You know you have ADD, right?...You've probably always had it." I looked at her and smiled and said "Thank GOD!"

She gave me Adderall, and it immediately changed my life. What a blessing! I love my ADD. I was soooo happy to have a valid explanation for the "WHY?!!!" I couldn't have done what I did thus far without ADD...and what I am going to do in the future. The Adderall helps me focus, gives me energy to get out of bed in the morning, instead of the afternoon, and I get so much more work done.

I worked at a restaurant for 8 years before my catering business, which I have owned for 10 years. I just sold my catering business

2 years ago and took a year off to write a book (brain-dumped all of my thoughts) and then got bored, so I called the restaurant and said "got any room for a retired caterer?" They brought me on as Marketing Manager for a year (I increased catering and banquet sales by 30%), and just recently got the position of Corporate Public Relations manager for both locations! It's my dream job - it's what I was meant to do. I feel like I've been in training for the last 10 years for this. I still get the freedom of working from home and being mobile, freely expressing my ideas (the entrepreneurial brain), and implementing them to help my company soar! So amazing!

Summary

We all have unique gifts that we present to the world, and the world needs all of our gifts to function properly. People who have a 4.0 GPA were given a very unique genetic gift of retention and recall, so they score very well on tests and are considered "book smart." People with AD/H tend to have a lower GPA, but were given a very unique genetic gift of creativity, ingenuity and fearlessness (as just a few of many great traits). They traditionally do not do as well at testing but think very quickly on their feet and are normally considered very "street smart."

Both are primarily genetic, both are unique gifts and both are very smart, but in their own unique ways. Why does one have to be so right and the other have to be so wrong? Why is it that one is considered to be the template for how we want all kids to be, and the other is considered a disorder? Why is it that one gift makes children feel so good while the other gift makes children feel so bad? Why does one gift build confidence in children while the other gift crushes confidence in children?

Why are we trying to turn every child into a 4.0 GPA student when it is an impossible goal? We are currently setting our children, parents, teachers, administrators and education system up for failure because we have given everyone an impossible mission. Genetics will never allow for every child to have a good memory and score well on tests. Can we do a better job of educating our children? Sure we can and we should always try. But today's measure of "smart" is inaccurate, misguided and cruel to our children. It is killing our children's confidence at epidemic rates, but we will keep letting it happen unless a dramatic shift of thinking occurs.

I don't think that anyone would disagree with the idea that confidence is one of the most critical ingredients in building successful careers and personal lives. Success allows people to feel confident in themselves and their decisions. It motivates them to take more emotional risks, which breeds even greater success. Quite the opposite, a lack of confidence makes you question yourself; it erodes your self-image and inhibits you from making powerful decisions for your life. You end up making emotionally safe decisions for yourself, which keeps you from greatness. Uncertainty kills dreams, especially uncertainty about ourselves.

Success is not necessarily about being smarter; it's all about believing in yourself. If the education system does not think you are "smart enough," and your parents do not think you are "smart enough" then how can you possibly believe in yourself? Confidence is what everyone needs to be emotionally healthy – let's work to rebuild it in our children, and even adults who still struggle with the insecurities that came along with poor grades in school. I also believe that every child that is struggling in school should be quickly evaluated by the school for AD/H or other possible learning challenges, so treatments can be sought before the child gets too far behind in their development.

I believe there are more than 150 million adults today with low self-worth issues related to their experience with our education system. Most are embarrassed to this very day and feeling inadequate because they did not get good grades in school. Or they are angry because they were so poorly judged and scored by a system that was incapable of seeing the truth of their brilliance. This huge part of our population has emotional wounds that go very deep, and they will continue to suffer in silence until something is done to admit our current traditional public education system's shortcomings.

It is time to break the silence, tell the truth and let the healing begin. If you are AD/H, then you are not dumb; you are not broken; you are not disordered; you are a perfect you. The grading system is what is broken, and it must be fixed. We need to redefine what "smart" is and hold our education system accountable for making sure that our children walk away from our schools with their head held high and excitement in their hearts about their incredibly bright future – every child deserves hope.

I also want greater awareness of AD/H because I believe the statistics for the number of people who have AD/H are grossly under-estimated. I believe it is closer to 30 percent, which would answer a lot of questions as to why so many of our children are under a 2.70 GPA and are dropping out of school at an alarming rate. Over the years, I have watched the experts estimate how many of our children have AD/H, and it started at 3 percent about ten years ago, then went to 5 percent, then 7 percent, then some say 10 percent, and today I saw a report that says it could be 12 percent. The fact is most children are not evaluated and diagnosed, so as awareness grows, so will the number of diagnoses.

A new study (2012) that was authored by Dr. Darios Getahun, a scientist for Kaiser Permanente Southern California Health Plan, proves my point. In 843,000 children ages 5 to 11, between 2001 and 2010, rates of new AD/HD diagnoses skyrocketed 24 percent. Rates went up most among minority children during the study period, climbing nearly 70 percent overall in black children and 60 percent among Hispanic youth. Among black girls, ADHD rates jumped 90 percent. Rates remain highest in white children. The biggest factor driving this increase may be the heightened awareness of ADHD among parents, teachers and pediatricians says the study's lead author.

This study brings up another problem. Is it possible that only children, who have the parents with the financial resources to pay for an evaluation, are being diagnosed with AD/H? Is that the reason that the experts have such low numbers in estimating the number of children with AD/H? It sure stands to reason that most of the underdiagnosed are from families who cannot afford a psychiatrist to perform the evaluation process. Even if they were diagnosed, could they afford the treatment option available to them, whether it is medication, coaching, or specialized schooling? A friend of mine told me that he and his wife pay $1,000 a month to have one of their sons in special classes to help him cope with his learning challenges associated with AD/H. How many people have that kind of money? This is certainly going to exacerbate the income gap between the affluent and non-affluent.

I believe that every child that is struggling should be evaluated by the school for AD/H, so treatments can be sought before the child gets too far behind in their development. We should remove the word "disorder" from the diagnoses because it serves no one but the medical community, and even they don't need it. Why not just identify children as "Attention Deficit" or "Hyperactive?" No child should ever be made to feel disordered or "not good enough." People with AD/H may be "differently ordered" but we are not "disordered" – the label is a confidence killer. If those of us with AD/H are disordered because we have a deficit in attention, then everyone has a disorder of some type because everyone has a deficit of something.

About the Author

Brad Worthley is the founder of Brad Worthley International, Inc., a Bellevue, Washington based consulting, coaching and training firm. An accomplished consultant with more than 39 years of business management experience, he is also an internationally acclaimed leadership, customer service and motivational expert. He has written four books and trained hundreds of thousands of people throughout a wide range of industries throughout the world. A true professional, Brad equips companies with dynamic customer service, leadership and motivational essentials. He teaches leading corporations how to consistently build and retain both customer and employee loyalty using his proven methods.

He is a master storyteller and delivers his powerful message from the customer's perspective with passion and humor. Many have referred to his lively presentations as "shows." Brad is always one of the highest rated speakers at any event he speaks at, and the common response from attendees is: *"When will he be back!"*

After college and an Associate of Science degree, Brad started his business career at the age of 20 by opening a sporting goods store. Since then, he has created and sold six other successful businesses in the fields of retail, wholesale, marketing, distribution and consulting. He has experienced every aspect of the business world, and not only talks the talk, but walks the walk.

Brad Worthley International produces training DVDs on customer service, leadership and motivation, which are being used by organizations from all industries and all sizes throughout the world, as well as many audio programs and books. Brad writes two monthly electronic newsletters called "Insights and Strategies" which have thousands of loyal subscribers in over 100 countries (you can subscribe at www. BradWorthley.com).

Brad is a past President (2002/2003) of the Mystery Shopping Providers Association, whose goal is dedicated to improving customer service. He received the "Volunteer of the Year Award" for 2001, and in 2002, was honored with the "Hall of Fame" award, the highest honor in the industry.

For more information on his services, product, articles and resources, visit Brad Worthley on-line at www.BradWorthley.com or www.Iam-NotDisordered.com, join Brad on www.Facebook.com/BradWorthley or follow him at www.Twitter.com/BradWorthley.

Brad Worthley International, Inc.
12819 SE 38th St. #375
Bellevue, WA 98006
(425)957-9696
Brad@BradWorthley.com

Helpful Resources

ADD is a Gift, not a Disorder website
 http://www.IamNotDisordered.com

WebMD
 http://www.webmd.com/add-adhd

Children and adults with Attention Deficit / Hyperactivity Disorder
 http://www.CHADD.org

National Resource Center for ADHD
 http://www.help4adhd.org

ADHD Management.com
 http://adhdmanagement.com

Own Your ADD
 http://www.ownyouradd.com

Attention Deficit Disorder Association
 http://www.add.org

ADHD Coaches Organization (ACO)
 http://www.adhdcoaches.org

National Study Group on Chronic Disorganization
http://www.nsgcd.org

National Association of Professional Organizers
http://napo.net

National Institute for Mental Health
http://www.nimh.nih.gov

National Center for Learning Disabilities
http://www.ncld.org

Inside ADHD
http://www.InsideADHD.org

LD OnLine
http://www.ldonline.org

ADD on About.com
http://add.about.com

HealthCentral.com
http://www.healthcentral.com/adhd

ADDitude Magazine
http://www.additudemag.com

ADHD and You
http://www.adultadhdisreal.com

ADDA Twitter Page
http://twitter.com/adultadhd

ADDClasses
http://ADDclasses.com

Virtual ADHD Conference
http://www.adhdconference.com

ADHD Family Online
http://www.adhdfamilyonline.com

ADDvance
  http://www.addvance.com

ADD Consults
  http://www.ADDconsults.com

ADD Warehouse
  http://www.addwarehouse.com

Living with ADD
  http://livingwithadd.com

Other books from Brad Worthley that are available at www.BradWorthley.com:

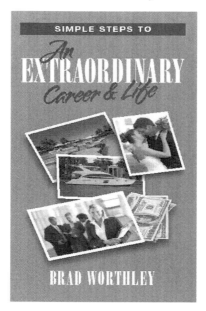

"Simple Steps to an Extraordinary Career & Life" will help you:

- Excel in your career
- Achieve happiness in your life
- Create remarkable relationships
- Enjoy a more stress free and productive life
- Accomplish goals you never thought possible

Why do so many people want to be promoted into management, be the top performing salesperson, lose weight, stop smoking, get rich, build their dream home, own a yacht or simply have a great relationship, but only a small percentage ever achieve it? That is because everyone has an inner saboteur trying to keep you from reaching your goals. This book will teach you the simple steps to have the things in life that you truly want. Achieving your desires is not about your I.Q., your grade-point in school, your childhood, the amount of money you have today or how lucky you are. You can have an extraordinary career and life if you choose, and this book will show you how, regardless of your past.

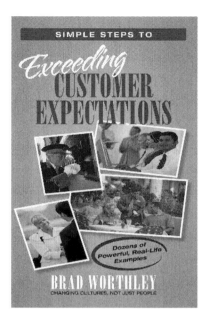

"Exceeding Customer Expectations will help you:
- Create and sustain a strong service culture
- Understand exactly what "exceed" look like
- Improve customer perceptions of your business
- Increase profits by increasing service standards
- Change customers from apathetic to advocates

Simply meeting the customer's expectations creates a base of customers who are apathetic (not loyal). If your competition offers a better value, these customers will abandon you. The goal must be to exceed each customer's expectations so that we create advocates. Advocates are not only fiercely loyal, but they also become promoters and tell other people about you.

This book is about how everyone we interact with should be treated with ultimate respect: customers, co-workers and vendors. Brad provides you with dozens of real-life examples of employees and businesses that have exceeded their customer's expectations and created lasting memories. This book is a must read for all employees, in all industries, regardless of their job responsibilities.

"Speaking of Success" will help you:

- Learn different paths to success
- What makes a great leader successful
- How to influence others with your behavior
- Find the true you in your journey to happiness
- Be a not only a better leader, but be a better person

This book is a compilation of experts such as Ken Blanchard, Stephen Covey, Jack Canfield (Chicken Soup for the Soul books), Brad Worthley and many others. Brad's 22 pages of the book define the role of leaders and how they can either make or break a service culture. This is Brad's first written offering on the importance of moving from being a manager to a leader. This is a must have!

Please visit our website and store where you can find t-shirts and mugs with some of these fun slogans on them. They will make great gifts for friends, family and co-workers (OK, and yourself too).

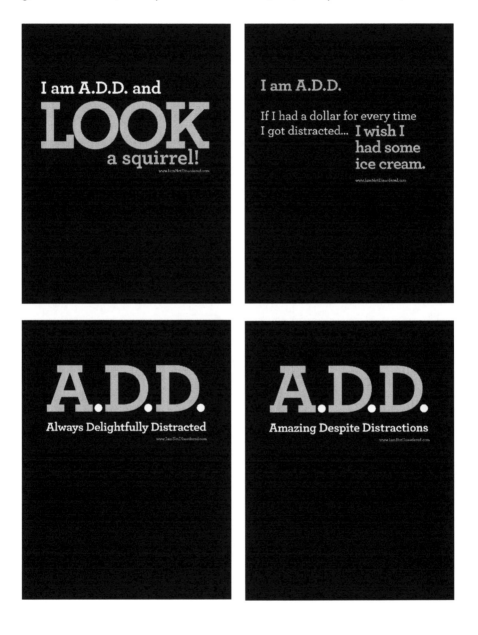

Please make sure to visit our website:

www.IamNotDisordered.com

where we have many additional resources available to you:

- A **FREE** AD/HD Survey (to see if you may have the gift)
- Helpful Video Clips
- A Blog to Share Your Thoughts
- T-Shirts with Fun A.D.D. Slogans
- Mugs with Fun A.D.D. Slogans

Made in the USA
Charleston, SC
21 May 2013